Develop your NLP Skills

D0320604

THE SUNDAY TIMES

Develop your NLP Skills

Andrew Bradbury | Fourth Edition

KoganPage

LONDON   PHILADELPHIA   NEW DELHI

Publisher's note

Every possible effort has been made to ensure that the information contained in this book is accurate at the time of going to press, and the publishers and authors cannot accept responsibility for any errors or omissions, however caused. No responsibility for loss or damage occasioned to any person acting, or refraining from action, as a result of the material in this publication can be accepted by the editor, the publisher or the author.

First edition published in 1997 as *NLP for Business Success*
Second edition published in 2000 as *Develop Your NLP Skills*
Third edition 2006
Fourth edition 2010

120 Pentonville Road	525 South 4th Street, #241	4737/23 Ansari Road
London N1 9JN	Philadelphia PA 19147	Daryaganj
United Kingdom	USA	New Delhi 110002
www.koganpage.com		India

© Andrew J Bradbury, 1997, 2000, 2006, 2010

ISBN   978 0 7494 5661 0
E-ISBN 978 0 7494 5930 7

The views expressed in this book are those of the author and are not necessarily the same as those of Times Newspapers Ltd.

British Library Cataloguing in Publication Data

A CIP record for this book is available from the British Library.

Library of Congress Cataloging-in-Publication Data

Bradbury, Andrew (Andrew J.)
    Develop your NLP skills / Andrew Bradbury. -- 4th ed.
        p. cm.
    ISBN 978-0-7494-5661-0 -- ISBN 978-0-7494-5930-7 1. Communication in management-- Psychological aspects. 2. Neurolinguistic programming. 3. Self-actualization (Psychology) 4. Success in business. I. Title.
    HD30.3.B687 2010
    158.1--dc22

                                                                            2009043257

Typeset by Jean Cussons Typesetting, Diss, Norfolk
Printed and bound in India by Replika Press Pvt Ltd

Contents

Introduction

Not so common sense

Right at the start I'd like to clear up a common misconception about NLP-related techniques, such as those I'm going to describe here, which will also explain the title of this book.

The most common misconception is that many NLP-related techniques are based on nothing more than common sense, to which we might reply, 'Yes, they are indeed based on so-called common sense. Only it appears common sense isn't nearly as "common" as many people seem to imagine.'

To explain what I mean I'd like to paraphrase a comment by Edward de Bono (inventor of Lateral Thinking), found in the Introduction to his book *Practical Thinking* (1971):

> The value of naming and describing the patterns identified in the development of NLP and the related techniques lies in making them recognizable. It then becomes possible to recognize these patterns in your own thinking and behaviour, and in the thinking and behaviour of others. You can also talk about them in as definite a way as you might talk about a car or a hamburger. Without those named patterns,

however, thinking in this area tends to be vague and intangible and hence very difficult to talk about.

As soon as you can talk about this subject you are on the way to regarding it as a skill, like playing tennis or cooking. And to regard it as a skill rather than as a gift is the first step towards doing something to improve that skill.

Far from being a matter of common sense, as de Bono said about thinking skills in general:

> Far too many people regard thinking as a matter of inborn intelligence – which it is not. In my researches and experiments I have again and again come across very intelligent people who turned out to be very poor thinkers. Nor have I found that thinking skill has much to do with education, for some of the best educated people (PhDs, university lecturers and professors, senior business executives, etc) have also been poor thinkers.

Practical Thinking, pp 8-9

(To see just how accurate de Bono's observations were, see http:// www.bradburyac.mistral.co.uk/nlpfax28.htm for example.) It is a basic tenet of NLP that whilst we aren't born with the full set of NLP-related skills, most people can become as adept as they wish to be, depending on how much time and effort they are willing to devote to learning and practising those skills.

This book will provide you with a grounding in some of the basic and most important skills associated with NLP, particularly, but definitely not exclusively, as they can be used in a business context. Then it will be down to you to build on that initial expertise by gaining experience in using the skills through practice and, if you are willing to make the commitment, by attending relevant training courses.

For the moment, congratulations on taking this step towards further developing your personal skill set.

1

Modelling

That name

NLP, as you may already know, stands for Neuro-Linguistic Programming (with hyphen). According to the most plausible account, it got that name when Richard Bandler, the originator and co-creator of NLP, was pulled over by a Highway Patrolman and asked for his details, including his occupation. Bandler was actually a student at the University of California, Santa Cruz at the time, but being in a somewhat whimsical mood he paused, scanned the titles of the text books lying on the seat beside him, and came up with 'Neuro-Linguistic Programmer'. And he liked the title so much that he kept it. On page two of *NLP Volume 1*, (Dilts, Grinder, Bandler and DeLozier, Meta Publications 1980), the authors explain that:

> 'Neuro' ... stands for the fundamental tenet that all behaviour is the result of neurological processes. 'Linguistic' ... indicates that neural processes are represented, ordered and sequenced into models and strategies through language and communication systems. 'Programming' refers to the process of organizing the components of a system (sensory representations in this case) to achieve specific outcomes.

That is to say, since our behaviour is based on our neurology (the activity in our brains), and we can organise our neurology by the way we use language, so it is possible to deliberately alter (programme, or re-programme) our behaviour through the use of communication in general and language in particular.

In 2009 that may seem like mere common sense. Back in the 1970s, however, brain scanning technology was still pretty new, and we knew a great deal less about the workings of the brain than we do now. These ideas were really quite radical then, especially given that they were based on Bandler and Grinder's observations and innovative thinking rather than on conventional laboratory experimentation.

The NLP quartet

We now come to a sort of secret. Not a very well kept secret, I grant you. In fact it wasn't meant to be a secret at all, a situation co-creator of NLP, John Grinder, did his best to resolve in his book *Whispering in the Wind* (J&C Enterprises, 2001). And the 'secret' is this: What many people think of as NLP isn't just one thing at all. There are, in fact, three elements in all, or four, if we include NLP-related training. The four elements are:

- **The 'field' of NLP, which covers all of the other three elements, plus all the people 'doing' NLP.**
- **NLP itself, which is a single, clearly defined, modelling process, and nothing else.**
- **The NLP-related techniques/applications which have been created, adopted and adapted primarily as tools which support the modelling process and/or which grew out of the use of the NLP modelling process.**
- **Effective NLP training passes on, within reason, not only descriptions of NLP techniques, but also understanding of how and when to utilise them.**

In practice the first three elements often get treated as a single entity, even in NLP circles. As John Grinder commented:

> If we adopt the common usage of the term NLP, the critical point concerning modelling is lost. If we insist on the distinction between NLP [modelling] and NLP [application], we are swimming upstream in the river of usage.
>
> *Whispering in the Wind*, p 51

So what is 'NLP modelling'? What differentiates it from any other type of modelling?

Whose model is it anyway?

In this context, the purpose of modelling is to take a skill possessed by one person – the exemplar – and create a description which will make it possible to incorporate that skill into your own and/or other people's skill set. And we choose one person rather than another because the person we choose as the exemplar is usually the person most highly rated, by their peers, in regard to the skill we want to model.

Isn't it strange, then, that most skill-modelling techniques focus as much, or even more, on the modeller rather than on the exemplar? That is to say, in most cases the modeller has direct, conscious influence over what does or doesn't go into the final model. And it is usually the modeller who decides when the model is complete. Authentic NLP modelling, as we will see in a moment, follows a significantly different route.

What is '(the) unconscious'?

Another important point that needs to be made clear is what we mean, in the context of NLP, by the term 'unconscious'. Much of the confusion about the 'unconscious brain' is caused by:

1   the way people tend to talk about it as the 'unconscious' or 'subconscious' mind, which many people think of as being something other than the brain;
2   the idea that 'unconscious' always means 'dead to the world';
3   the mistaken belief that NLPers share Freud's belief in the unconscious as a storage facility for undesirable thoughts.

In practice, however, when we talk about the unconscious or subconscious brain all we mean is that area of the brain that we aren't consciously aware of at any given moment.

We might also note that NLPers have long believed that the unconscious brain is better at a number of tasks that humans regularly perform, because it does not get bogged down in all the 'shoulds', 'oughts' and 'musts' – not to mention all the things we think we know but don't – which regularly send us off course when we think we are making 'rational' decisions.

Whilst this was also based on observation rather than experimentation, it is interesting that evidence is now appearing which supports this view. See, for example, 'Unconscious Decisions' and 'Our Unconscious Brain Makes The Best Decisions Possible', online at: http://www.sciencedaily.com/releases/2008/12/081224215542.htm and http://www.scientificamerican.com/article.cfm?id=unconscious-decisions.

Communicating with the unconscious

Following on from this, the notion of 'unconscious' or 'implicit' *learning* simply means 'learning without intending to learn, and/or without knowing, at a conscious level, that any learning is taking place'. This may sound a trifle odd, until you remember that this is the first form of learning any of us ever uses – when we're learning to walk and talk, for example. No one sits us down and says, 'OK, kid – now you learn to talk!' What really happens is that we learn implicitly – by modelling other people's behaviour. We 'pick it up as we go along', by watching and listening to whoever we spend most time with. Which is why, as children at least, most of us have roughly the same accent and vocabulary as other members of our own family. (Brain elements known as 'mirror neurons' may possibly help to explain what is going on here, but see below.)

By the same token, several NLP-related techniques involve 'talking to someone's "unconscious brain"', which may also seem like a strange idea, first time around. Yet the fact is that we do it all the time. That is to say, we regularly talk to our own unconscious brain (self-talk), and to the unconscious part of other people's brains. Since the 'unconscious brain' is simply the part of the brain we aren't currently consciously aware of, it surely follows that it is nevertheless always present. What our conscious brain hears our unconscious brain also hears. So here is the point of this discussion: our unconscious brain learns extremely well from our day-to-day experiences, not least because it has equal access to all of our senses, but without imposing existing beliefs and filters on what it takes in.

Unconscious modelling

Say a company wanted to train up a group of graduate recruits as sales people. The process would need to start from the ground up. And part of the training would be to develop a good, conscious knowledge of the company's line of products. But what about the acquisition of sales skills?

One approach might be to ask one of the sales team to spend some time in the training room, giving the trainees a detailed account of the work that he or she does.

The problem with that is that asking a salesperson, or anyone else who is an expert at what they do, to pass on their core skill to other people can be a spectacular failure, simply because most experts have little or no conscious awareness of how they manage to be successful.

There is, for example, the story of 'Tom', a top salesman who was sure that he had achieved this position because of his encyclopaedic knowledge of the products he dealt in. For every question clients put to him he always had the answer.

Yet when someone from the company asked some of Tom's customers about this, they all said that they preferred dealing with Tom because he always showed a very genuine interest in their families, remembering anniversaries, birthdays, etc.

Alternatively, we could have someone follow one of the most successful members of the sales team around for a number of days, taking in (modelling) everything the sales person does and then passing that information to the trainees.

But here again there is a problem with non-NLP forms of modelling – in that the modeller may inadvertently overlook or exclude information that the trainees actually need. As Bandler and Grinder explained, in *Frogs into Princes*:

> We call ourselves modelers. What we essentially do is to pay very little attention to what people say they do and a great deal of attention to what they do... We have no idea about the 'real' nature of things, and we are not particularly interested in what's 'true.' The function of modeling is to arrive at descriptions which are useful.

p 7

The 'Know Nothing' State

The first step in using the NLP modelling process, then, is for the modeller to temporarily ignore any existing ideas they might have about what the exemplar does, how they do it, or why they do it. Obviously the modeller will consciously select what skill they want to acquire, and will consciously select who they wish to model in order to learn that skill. But having done that, the modeller must, when using the NLP technique, cease any attempt to consciously evaluate the exemplar's behaviour or select what aspects of that behaviour belongs in the final model. This they can do by adopting the 'Know Nothing State' in which they act and think as though they had absolutely no prior knowledge or experience of the skill they are modelling. By doing this, the modeller acquires an unabridged and untainted model of the exemplar's skill. (By the way, this is often the best way to collect accurate information in any context.)

That's the way to do it

Know nothing state 1

It must be said here, that many Westerners have difficulty accepting the value of the know nothing state, so here is a word of explanation:

> A man once approached the Khoja Nasruddin in the teahouse and asked to become his student.
>
> 'I have studied for many years, with many masters,' the man explained. 'And now I have come to learn from you.'
>
> The Khoja smiled and asked if the man would care for a cup of tea. When the man accepted Nasruddin took a cup and filled it to the brim. Then, as the man thanked him, Nasruddin asked again if he would care for a cup of tea.
>
> 'But Khoja,' the man replied, greatly mystified by the question, 'my cup is already full. There is no room for any more.'
>
> 'Quite so,' said Nasruddin.

So how do you create a 'know nothing state' at will?

You might argue that you cannot stop yourself from thinking. And you'd be absolutely right. So rather than trying to avoid doing something, you focus on some other activity which will achieve the required result. In this case you focus so intensely, moment-by-moment, on what the exemplar is doing that you don't have room to form conscious thoughts about it or analyse that behaviour.

I realise that having said that NLP modelling should be an unconscious process, it may seem a little odd to be saying 'focus moment-by-moment on what the other person is doing'. But it is precisely that moment-by-moment element which ensures that the process is effectively unconscious. I have used this approach myself for many years, during my time as an IT trainer. For several of the courses I ran I had to learn everything initially just by sitting in on three or four seminars, several weeks apart, presented by the person who had been running the course up till then. To consciously learn that much about a subject I previously knew nothing about, and learn it well enough to teach the material to experienced technical staff, would have been nigh on impossible in the short time available. So I would just focus all of my attention on the presenter and allow myself to take in everything that he or she said and did without making any attempt at all to understand or evaluate what the presenter was doing, or why.

Try it yourself

To get some idea of what that's like, here's a little experiment that you can do which will illustrate the point:

Next time you are walking down the street, start watching someone in front of you (someone you don't already know), with your complete attention (other than what you need to avoid bumping in to other people). Don't let anything intrude on your focus, not even your own thoughts. At the same time, begin to copy the other person's way of walking – from head to toe. But make the imitation subtle rather than 'life size'. This is just an illustration, not full blown modelling.

Again this is nothing like as strange as it may seem to be. If you have the opportunity to observe a group of people whilst they are watching a film or a TV programme, you will invariably find that most members of the group are to some extent or other physically yet unconsciously reflecting what they are seeing on the screen. In my own case, as a very enthusiastic, and reasonably competent cross-country runner in my school days I still find it quite impossible to sit completely still whilst watching long distance running on TV. So if you're tempted to take an active part in creating a know nothing state, just relax, it will come all by itself if you allow it to happen.

And now, a last thought on the experiment. If you get distracted when watching that other person, just notice, briefly, how you had to break out of that fully-focused state in order to have a conscious thought about whatever you were focused on. Then return to being fully focused.

Know nothing state 2

The second approach is more or less the direct opposite of the first method, and can be illustrated by the story of how one of NLP's co-creators modelled therapist Virginia Satir when she was conducting a lengthy training course featuring her own particular approach to family therapy.

Richard Bandler was running the sound and recording systems for Satir, but without paying very much attention to what was happening in the training room (he had his headphones wired up so he could listen to Satir in one ear, and music by bands like Pink Floyd in the other). Nonetheless, on one occasion when the trainees seemed completely stumped over a situation set up by Satir, Bandler left the control booth, went down to the training area, and not only resolved the stand-off but did it in a way that Satir herself agreed was entirely consistent with her approach.

How, then, had Bandler acquired the skills needed to achieve this result? Through a process of 'unconscious acquisition' or 'implicit learning'.

Here again the process makes perfectly good sense if recent discoveries regarding 'mirror neurons' are correct. According to Dr Suresh Muthukumaraswamy of Cardiff University, mirror neurons are activated when we watch specific actions, even when we are concentrating on some other activity. Given that much of Satir's work involved physical actions and the relationships between people as expressed by arranging family members in tableaux, Muthukumaraswamy's description seems to bear a clear resemblance to the way in which Bandler learnt from Satir.

> **Note: Although research on 'mirror neurons' began back in the mid-1990s, it must be emphasised that this research is still in its infancy and not everyone interested in this area is yet convinced that what are called mirror neurons actually fulfil the functions attributed to them.**

The method

If then, in the example of the graduate recruits, we were to apply the NLP approach, we would start by finding a skilled modeller to 'shadow' the exemplar – one of the company's top salespeople – over a period of time, literally 'for as long as it takes'.

The modeller will obviously know, consciously, who they are modelling, and what skill they wish to model. But from that point on the actual modelling must be conducted at the subconscious level. That is to say, the modeller should make no attempt whatever to consciously analyse or evaluate the salesperson's behaviour. Because by doing so they may filter out or distort information which is an essential element of the exemplar's skill. In fact, for that same reason the modeller will not even ask questions about what the salesperson is doing, though they may mimic the exemplar's behaviour (in a covert manner so that it is not apparent to anyone else who is present).

Remember: the modelling should only be conducted in appropriate contexts – in this case only when and where the sales person is actually interacting with a customer, whether face-to-face or on the phone, or planning/reflecting on such a meeting. (Modelling face-to-face behaviour might be managed by introducing the modeller as someone new to the sales force who has simply come out to meet some of the company's customers.)

This goes on, with the modeller building up an unconscious, experience-based model of what the exemplar actually does and says, neither consciously accepting or rejecting any additional information that comes up (such as perceptions, values and beliefs), until the modeller can genuinely and successfully perform as a salesperson in a manner that replicates the exemplar's results. The modeller's competence, or otherwise, in these tests should be assessed from feedback. The modeller him/herself should not try to evaluate their own performance.

Once the modeller can replicate the exemplar's results the modelling itself stops. But this is not the end of the overall process.

Refining the model

What the modeller now has is a fairly exact model of a specific person using their skill. But what they actually want is only the aspects of the person's performance which are necessary to their success. Thus unless they actually deal in some aspect of home entertainment, the fact that the salesperson has over 2,000 DVDs may be true without necessarily having any bearing whatever on their sales success.

Once an effective model has been created, all of its elements must be individually tested to determine whether they are actually necessary for the success of the model.

To refine the model, then, the modeller needs to try out the model removing one element at a time in a series of role plays. If the absence of a given element can be seen to make a negative difference to the modeller's performance then it is relocated as part of the model before any other elements are tested.

If, on the other hand, removing an element seems to make no difference to the modeller's success then it is permanently removed from the model.

Teaching the model

If the model were being created purely for use by the modeller there would be no further work to do. However, since the model is to be used in the training of the graduates when it has been reduced to the minimum amount of detail which still supports a fully effective performance, it must be 'documented' in such a way that it can be accurately transmitted to the trainees so that they, too, can learn to replicate the exemplar's performance.

A simple written description will suffice, though it might incorporate certain NLP-related techniques, such as sub modalities, presuppositions, etc, to give a more concise picture.

And that is NLP. Now for the rest.

2

Thinking NLP

Taken as read

Whenever we interact with other people and/or with our environment, we do so on the basis of a whole multitude of presuppositions – assumptions about what is, or is not, true in a given situation.

In most cases these assumptions are based on prior experience of some kind. For example, when you get out of bed first thing in the morning, do you first look over the edge of the bed to check that there is a floor for you to stand on? Or do you simply take it for granted that the floor will be exactly where you left it the night before? And how time consuming would it be if you never made any assumptions but checked everything as though you had no prior experience to go on? (Sadly we know, from observing cases of Alzheimer's disease, how crippling this approach would be.)

So presuppositions are a very useful, even essential, part of everyday life. But even some of the presuppositions we most readily take for granted are not necessarily correct. Another common, but far less easily justified presupposition says that if you and I speak the same language then we will both attach the same meanings to the words we use. In reality, however, language is a comparatively unreliable resource, and we can quickly see the weakness of the assumption of shared meaning if we start trying to find universally agreed definitions for words like 'nice', 'beautiful', 'clever', 'justice' and 'education'.

NLP – Neuro-Linguistic Programming – has its own underlying presuppositions. Depending on who you listen to, or read, there is now a fairly flexible list of anything up to about 25 different presuppositions, from which each NLP-oriented writer and training organisation has tended to select those entries which they believe express the most important aspects of NLP's core philosophy.

I have chosen those presuppositions which I believe are particularly relevant to the use of NLP in the business environment so that you can immediately get some idea of the thinking that underlies the techniques and methods you will be reading about in the rest of the book.

The presuppositions

Context makes meaning

We sometimes assume that things going on around us have a single, universal meaning. This presupposition proposes that 'meaning' is actually a mental construct (it exists in the mind of the perceiver, rather than in what is being perceived). And because meaning is linked to perception, it is determined by the context within which the perception occurs. When someone comes towards you holding a knife, it makes a real difference whether you are in your own kitchen and the person holding the knife is preparing food or whether it's in a dark alley and the person with the knife is demanding your money.

Every behaviour has a positive intention

This is possibly the most controversial of the NLP presuppositions, since it is so open to misinterpretation. What the presupposition means in the context of NLP is that every behaviour has a positive intention, *as far as the person exhibiting the behaviour is concerned.*

Can we really transpose such a *seemingly* idealistic concept to the business-place? George M Prince, writing in the *Harvard Business Review* some three years before the very first book on NLP was published, gives an excellent example of how this notion might be applied in management. He lists various 'contrasting assumptions' that make the difference between a negative, critical manager and a positive, supportive manager, including:

Judgmental Manager
When subordinates express themselves or act in ways unacceptable to me, I point out the flaws.

Judicious Manager
When subordinates express themselves or act in unacceptable ways, I assume they had reasons that made sense to them and explore the action from that point of view.

It is worth pointing out here that NLP does not claim that all behaviour is necessarily the best possible choice from an *objective* point of view. Nor does it suggest that all behaviour will have positive benefits for *everyone* involved.

Every behaviour is appropriate in some context

If we repeat a certain pattern of behaviour it is usually because once upon a time it produced a desired result. The trouble is that we often go on using some patterns even when, from an outsider's viewpoint, they are manifestly no longer appropriate. By implication, the most effective solution to unwanted behaviour is to find a more appropriate alternative rather than holding a lengthy, pointless post-mortem over the old behaviour (which is more likely to reinforce that old behaviour).

People will normally make the best choice available to them in any given situation

As well as having a positive intention, people will base their behaviour on *what seems to them* to be the best choice out of whatever choices they perceive as being available to them. At least two important influences are at work here.

Firstly, 'context makes meaning', but context itself is a matter of perception, and a person may perceive context A as being much like context B when, from an objective point of view, any similarities are purely superficial. Thus someone behaving inappropriately may simply have misunderstood the context.

Secondly, we have also seen that people will often repeat behaviour because it once worked, regardless of whether they see the past and present contexts as being similar.

In other words, no matter how calculating and rational we may try to be, making choices is a very subjective process, and what looks like a 'best' choice to one person may look like quite a poor choice to someone else.

The key issue is that few people ever deliberately, knowingly make a 'bad' choice.

A map is not the territory it depicts; words are not the things they describe; symbols are not the things they represent

'A map is not the territory' was originally coined by Alfred Korzybski (the founder of General Semantics):

> A map *is not* the territory it represents, but, if correct, it has a *similar structure* to the territory, which accounts for its usefulness.
>
> *Science and Sanity*, 5th edn, 1994, IGS, Englewood, NJ, p 58, italics as in the original

In practical terms, this presupposition expresses the notion that we can never know everything there is to know about anything, no matter how simple. In order to make sense of the world around us, then, we 'draw' our own set of 'mental maps', but always on the basis of a selected subset of all possible information (just as a 'map' is not the landscape it depicts but merely a very limited subset of all possible information about that particular piece of the landscape).

People respond to their internal maps of reality, not to reality itself

At this point we can draw together the various concepts we've looked at so far and clear up a fairly widespread misunderstanding in the process. For the last 2,000 years and more, Western thinking has been in thrall to Aristotle's brand of two-valued thinking, which basically assumes that there is one right solution to every problem and everything else is wrong, that there is just one right view of any situation and every other view is wrong, and so on. This particular presupposition says that there are multiple possibilities in any problem (of varying degrees of utility), a variety of viewpoints in any situation, etc, because each person will have their own perceptions and in practice they will respond to those perceptions rather than to the objective reality that triggered those perceptions.

In contrast to Aristotelian thinking, this NLP concept of 'personal perception' is closer to the solipsistic teaching that predominated before Socrates, Plato and Aristotle started to rock the philosophical boat. There are, however, at least two varieties of solipsism, rather than just one, namely *epistemological* solipsism and *metaphysical* solipsism.

Epistemological solipsism, which is the viewpoint NLP is based upon, does not deny the existence of an external, 'absolute' reality; it simply says that each of us has an internal representation of that reality, which is what we base our thoughts and behaviour on. Metaphysical solipsism, which some writers have (wrongly) assumed NLP supports, holds that there is *no* external reality and that therefore everything is just a fantasy playing out in someone's mind. Just whose mind that might be is anybody's guess.

As one of Bob Dylan's lyrics has it, 'I'll let you be in my dream, if you'll let me be in yours.'

If you go on doing what you're doing now you are very likely to go on getting the same results as you are getting now

This is the first part of an optimistic presupposition, which emphasises the fact that, in *any* situation, we always have choices.

Though we may not be able to control what goes on in the world around us, we can *always* control how we *respond* to those events. If we always act/respond in the same way then the most likely result is that we will maintain the status quo.

If you want something different you must do something different, and keep varying your behaviour until you get the result that you want

The second part of the presupposition is that there are solutions to every situation if you're prepared to keeping on looking until you find them.

In a business context this points us to the fact that if change is required, then it had better be genuine change, not just an exercise in 'skilled incompetence', as Chris Argyris calls it – adopting new processes, but using old methods to carry them out (like trying to play a CD on a gramophone).

The person with the greatest number of choices in a given situation is most likely to achieve their outcome

Building on the previous presupposition, from an NLP viewpoint developing multiple options in any situation is seen as being more realistic than having only one or two. Indeed, from an NLP perspective:

- **One option is no choice at all.**
- **Two options is a dilemma.**
- **Real choice only starts when you have at least three options.**

Change makes change

It is a common saying that 'the only person you can really change is yourself'. NLP goes one step further and also acknowledges that changing your own behaviour inevitably has an effect on the people around you. The underlying notion, derived from cybernetics, is that when one element within a system changes, the whole system must change in order to adapt to that changed element. That 'system' may be your family and/or your friends and/or the people you work with, and so on, depending on what it is you decide to change.

You cannot *not* communicate

This presupposition simply makes the point that we are constantly communicating, both by what we do and by what we don't do, by what we say *and* by what we don't say, by the messages we send deliberately *and* by a host of mainly unconscious non-verbal signals.

Thus it is clearly in our own interest to understand the communication process as far as we can and to learn how to become effective communicators rather than simply leaving things to chance.

The meaning of your communication is the response that you get

The presupposition here is that people can only respond to what they *think* you mean, which may, or may not, be an accurate interpretation of your *intended* meaning.

(Please note: in this context, a 'communication' is the 'whole' message – not only what you *said* but also all of the accompanying non-verbal signals.)

What this presupposition explains is that, if we want people to respond appropriately to what we say, then we need to talk *to* them rather than *at* them. That is, we need to be constantly aware of other people's responses to what we're saying, and adjust our communication accordingly, rather than just assuming that they will have understood what we meant them to understand.

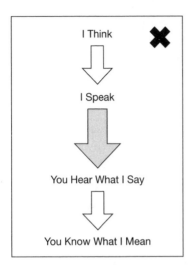
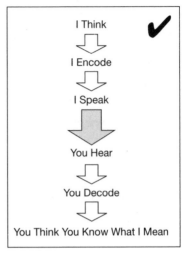

This presupposition does admittedly cause a certain amount of confusion on occasion. Quite a few people seem to think that it also means: 'Whatever *I think* your communication means must be what you *intended* it to mean.' This is an unjustified assumption and makes for poor communication.

Effective communication requires active participation on *both* sides. On the one hand it is certainly the responsibility of the person sending a message to check whether the message has been received and understood correctly, and to provide appropriate clarification if it hasn't. And it is the responsibility of the recipients of a message to indicate what clarification they need, if any, and to accept that clarification, even if it indicates a different meaning from the one in their initial interpretation.

Everyone has all of the resources they need

What this means is simply that a person is ultimately able to deal with any situation in which they may find themselves by drawing on their own inner resources (or capabilities), or by developing new resources, rather than by relying on someone or something else to give them a resource that they didn't previously have.

Having said that, according to *Bradbury's corollaries*, in order to use a resource you must:

- **know that you have it;**
- **know how to use it (though not necessarily at a *conscious* level).**

Genuine understanding only comes with experience

Whilst we can gain knowledge by a variety of routes – reading, talking, watching other people and so on – nothing is so completely educational, in a positive sense, as experience. You don't really *understand* something until you've done it yourself.

There is no such thing as failure, only feedback

When something doesn't go as we planned we often tend to see that as *failure*. Depending on the seriousness of the situation we might then get angry, irritated, sad, depressed, worried, guilty or whatever. None of which serves any useful purpose.

But what if we see the situation as *feedback* rather than *failure* – a demonstration of how not to do something? Instead of being wrong, we've learnt something. Instead of feeling bad, we are free to form a new plan of action and try again.

There is a story about a certain investment banker, one of whose assistants made a business decision that cost the company millions of dollars. When the assistant was called to the banker's office he expected to get a thorough roasting and quite possibly an invitation to seek new career opportunities – somewhere else.

'I'm so sorry, sir,' the young man exclaimed, as soon as he entered the banker's office. 'I wouldn't blame you one little bit if you fired me on the spot!'

'Fire you?' the banker answered, 'when it's cost the company several million dollars to train you in the finer points of risk management? Not a chance. I only called you in to make sure you'd learnt the lesson.'

Your brain and your body are indivisible parts of the same system

The notion that our body and our brain are separate entities seems to have developed within the medical profession in the 1930s and 1940s. If there was something wrong with the body – from a sniffle to malignant cancer – the only solution was some kind of physical treatment. And despite its position at the *head* of the central nervous system, in mainstream medicine it was received wisdom that the influence of the brain effectively stopped at the neck.

At the very same time, however, Alfred Korzybski and the General Semanticists were investigating the idea that mental activity had a direct correlation to physiological activity.

Only in the last couple of decades has practical, scientifically verifiable evidence come to light that shows beyond reasonable doubt that the immune system, for example, is integrally linked to brain activity, so that mental stress can inhibit the performance of the immune system and thus lead to a lowering of general physical health.

People aren't 'broken' and don't need to be 'fixed'

The old psychiatric metaphor put seemingly inappropriate

communications and/or behaviour on a par with a broken arm or leg. This led to the assumption that people could be mentally 'broken' and 'fixed' just as they could be physically broken and fixed. According to NLP, however, this is an inappropriate and misleading metaphor. W Edwards Deming ('father' of the Japanese industrial revolution) seems to have had a similar idea in mind when he offered this advice: 'If people don't get it, don't fix the people – fix the process.'

Checkpoint action

Pause from time to time in your everyday activities and notice what presuppositions you believe in.

For example, do you think that people are basically OK – trustworthy and capable of being loyal and responsible, even though they may need a little guidance from time to time? Or do you see people as being basically self-centred and untrustworthy and therefore in need of regular monitoring to ensure that they don't get up to something they shouldn't?

3

Points of view

Don't eat the menu

Our interactions with the external world are greatly influenced by our comparatively limited mental faculties. We receive millions of bits of data every minute (through our various senses), but we can only consciously handle a small fraction of that data grouped into 7 ± 2 chunks. The rest of the information is dealt with at the unconscious level. (A bit is a unit of data in information technology just as it is in computing.)

The process of abstracting a manageable picture from the mass of available data is often referred to in NLP as 'map-making'. Neuroscientist Professor Walter J. Freeman gives a succinct description of the basic map-making process in his book *How Brains Make Up Their Minds* (1999):

> ... the brain responds to the world by destabilizing the primary sensory cortices of the brain. The result is the construction of neural activity patterns, which provide the elements of which meaning is made. When the freshly made patterns are transmitted to other parts of the brain, the raw sense data that triggered them are washed away. What remains is what has been made within the brain.

(Please note that the terms 'maps' and 'map-making' are used throughout this chapter to refer specifically to mental maps.)

Not surprisingly, given so much information, no two people ever have *exactly* the same map in any situation. Even a single word can be the basis for two quite separate maps:

To make our communications more effective (and our relationships more harmonious) we need to be aware of both the strengths *and the limitations* of our maps. Becoming a mature person includes learning to accept the difference between 'this is true/not true' and 'this is true/not true *for me*'.

Bob criticised Jane's presentation because she had used bullet points on some of her slides and numbering in the handout. 'If you use numbers in the notes then you must use numbers on your slides', he insisted, 'that's the *proper* way to do it'.

Bob clearly understood how the numbered notes related to the bulleted slides, so it wasn't the numbering and bullet points as such that had caused the upset. The 'real problem' was that Jane's style was at odds with Bob's internal map of how things should be done. Bob missed the fact that there were thirty other people present, each of whom may also have had a view of what constituted a 'good presentation'. Yet all of the other people chose to put any such ideas to one side in order to get the most out of the presentation.

So Bob had a point about the inconsistency, but in practical terms he simply created an element of conflict, and reduced his own ability to find the presentation useful, enjoyable or informative by insisting that his map alone was valid.

So, we need to create these maps in order to make sense of the world around us, but we also need to be aware that even the best map is only a rough guide to the landscape it represents:

A Word		The THING it describes
A Map	**IS NOT**	The PLACE it depicts
A Symbol		The THING it represents

If maps were real we'd all be somewhere else!

Making mental maps is a natural process that kicks in even before we are born. It's how we store our life experience. As we get older we have more control over the process and sometimes, instead of making new maps we merely recycle the maps we already have. There are at least three reasons for creating new maps:

1. Maps are always based on a limited view of external reality, which is itself in a constant process of change.

2. The longer we use any particular map, the harder it becomes to recognise its shortcomings.
3. The more familiar a map becomes, the harder it is to accept the validity of anybody else's map of the same 'territory'.

And even when we do make new maps, they may be arrived at by evaluating any new information in the light of maps we have already prepared. This opens the door to three more ways of misunderstanding external reality:

1. **Generalisation**
   Assuming that something which applies to a specific situation will be equally appropriate everywhere else.
2. **Distortion**
   Editing our perceptions to create a more acceptable version of reality.
3. **Deletion**
   Ignoring information we don't like or can't be bothered with. Again to make it more acceptable.

Some typical (misleading) workplace maps include:

'A tidy desk shows a tidy mind' (Generalisation)
(Does a clear desk show an empty mind?)
'We expect our staff to behave in a professional manner' (Distortion)
(The definition of 'a professional' is someone who gets paid for what they do. However, this phrase often means 'We expect our staff to do unpaid overtime')
'Customers don't care about ...' (Deletion)
(Who says so? Where is the evidence?)

Checkpoint action

Listen to the conversations around you with the
following thoughts in mind:

- Are any generalisations, distortions or deletions
  being used?
- What assumptions is each person making?
- Are those assumptions justified?
- What do they tell you about the speakers' mental
  maps?
- What could you say to each speaker which would help
  them to understand other people's points of view?

4

Cultures, values and beliefs

Company map or virtual reality?

Strange but true, three of the most basic elements of company life – the company vision, the company mission and even company culture – are actually maps. What is more, calling them a 'company' vision and a 'company' mission is often highly misleading. (Interestingly, many families work to a similar arrangement.)

In the first place, many companies devise mission statements that are decidedly short on content, as can be seen in the example below, which appeared in a brochure put out by a major academic examination board:

> To facilitate the best methods of flexible and effective supervisory and management education, development and assessment.

It sounds terrific, but what does it mean?

Does any reputable company deliberately set out to use *second* best methods? 'Best', 'flexible' and 'effective' are all highly subjective words.

Who defined their methods as 'effective', and what yardstick was used?

As an indicator of the company's intentions this statement is a collection of buzzwords. As a 'map' it depicts a 'territory' that is little more than virtual reality.

All for one and...?

We need to recognise that a business map only has value if it embodies a *shared* reality. According to Alan Harrison at the School of Business Management, Brunel University: 'Behind the often bland facade of corporate communications, the language used encodes internal conflict and contradictions.' A survey by researchers at Brunel University showed that staff are beginning to decode company circulars and are turning against their employers as a result. 'They are particularly dismissive of the use of "we" to imply shared objectives,' says Harrison.

These findings would have been no surprise to the business commentator who observed:

> If your company mission has to be written down and passed around, you don't have a company mission.

Companies which ignore this message and rely on imposed maps will usually rely on a punitive, autocratic culture which leaves little room for individuality. They may flourish for a while, but sooner or later they begin to crumble. The process may not become terminal if the management style can be changed in time – by re-educating the existing management or by a major reorganisation. But the changes must be genuine, or the reorganisation itself may simply speed the collapse.

I originally wrote that last paragraph both as a generalisation and with a specific company in mind. Shortly after the second edition of this book came out, that company underwent the kind of major change that I described, including the removal of certain senior managers.

This emphasises the fact that company culture is usually set by senior management, and tends to change almost imperceptibly unless there is a major upheaval at that level.

Obviously these factors will have an impact throughout a company/organisation. If your working life seems unduly stressful, a worthwhile first step towards resolving the situation can be to review your own life maps, particularly your values and beliefs, in relation to your company's culture. A gradual drift into a new culture may have created a situation where you no longer share the prevailing value-set. Alternatively, the day-to-day running of the company may simply not match its declared mission and vision. In either case it may be that the simple act of identifying the mismatch is sufficient to ease the stress.

A matter of choice

Once upon a time, an American-owned software company in Britain was bought up by a British company which had quite extensive dealings with the MoD (Ministry of Defence). Only then did anyone discover that several top technicians – people whose presence had been a major reason for the purchase – had a distinct aversion to being involved with the military in any way, which they expressed by all leaving the company just a few weeks later. In that instance, the employees saw their situation as being *two-valued* – stay or leave. In most cases, however, it is more useful to view each situation from *multiple* standpoints, each with its own choice(s). Remember the NLP saying that you don't have a choice at all until you have at least *three* separate options to hand. Indeed, the most effective response is based on unlimited choices so that you can change even as the situation changes.

But what happens if you find that your personal values are at odds with those of your employer? Do you have to hand in your resignation, or put your personal beliefs to one side while you are at work? Not at all.

> If you go on doing what you're doing now, you'll go on getting what you're getting now.
>
> If you *want* something different, you have to change what you are *doing* until you get what you want.

One popular business model presents 'circles of influence' – clearly defined by two areas of influence; the area in which you can exert influence over what is going on, and everywhere else (where you have no influence). If we adopt this model we should never try to act outside our area of influence, because we will simply be wasting our time and energy. However, George Bernard Shaw nearly said:

> The reasonable man adapts himself to his circle of influence.
> The unreasonable one persists in trying to expand his circle of influence.
> Therefore all progress depends on the unreasonable man.

NLP goal setting (Chapter 8) tends to favour a more flexible view, based on what is influenceable, what is ecological and what is strategic:

- **Influenceable: Notice that this refers to what is 'influenceable', in general and/or by a particular person. In line with NLP's focus on increasing choices, this is based on the perception that we do not know how far our influence can extend unless we have the curiosity to push the boundaries (understanding through actual experience).**
- **Ecological: Only take time to exert influence where it will serve a useful purpose. Sometimes we can get so irritated or frustrated by a situation that, even though we know that it is really rather trivial or irrelevant or will take an undue amount of time and effort to resolve,**

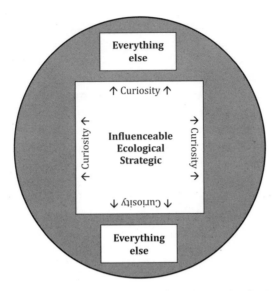

we get involved anyway. That is an *un*ecological
approach.

- **Strategic:** Using your influence to get results today is
fairly pointless if this approach generates more and/or
bigger problems in the future. Use influence where, so
far as you can tell, it will bring strategic (lasting)
benefits – or start building a pigeon loft right now for
when the birds come home to roost.

The pursuit of excellence

Nothing ever stays the same, and no business, large or small, can
ever afford to rest on its laurels. So, in a business context, the old
saying 'If it ain't broke, don't fix it' may not be the best policy.
There is certainly no point in adopting change for its own sake,
but any company that wants to stay ahead of the game must be
constantly checking its maps against the external situation, and
making appropriate adjustments when necessary.

Moreover, the process of change must be customised for each company. Beware the consultant who offers stock solutions to all of their clients. Some time ago certain 'experts' espoused Japanese work styles, but it soon turned out to be an approach that produced strictly limited success.

To be of practical use, a business map must take account of local customs, culture, social parameters, and especially of changing customer needs and expectations. What is true for Osaka may not be true for Tokyo, let alone for Detroit, Manchester or Hamburg. Squeezing a company into a particular business theory is like altering the landscape to fit a map. Generic business theories are fine, as long as they are recognised as such and are applied at the right level. There is a point at which the application of unmodified ideas automatically becomes counterproductive.

Checkpoint actions

1. To what extent does the management in your company act in accordance with the declared mission/vision?
2. As briefly as possible, how would you describe the culture in each of the companies you have worked for in the past?
3. From the list you drew up for question 2, what was particularly good or bad about each culture?
4. Using the assessments you made in question 3, what could you do to improve, or encourage improvement in, the culture of your present company?
5. List the three beliefs and three values which are most important in your life. Then discuss your selection with someone whose judgement you trust.

5

It all makes sense

What's really important?

Because we have a wealth of information coming in from the world around us, far more than we can handle at a conscious level, we tend to cope with the potential overload by filtering the information. One of the ways we filter is by selectively placing or focusing our attention, and one of the ways we can do that is by selecting which sensory channel(s) we will *pay most attention to*, even though we, of course, use *all* of our senses/rep' systems (sensory modes/representational systems) all of the time. In the context of NLP the five senses are often referred to as *representational systems* – visual (sight), auditory (sound), kinaesthetic (feelings, emotional and tactile), olfactory (smell) and gustatory (taste). Or VAKOG, for short. (By the way, this selecting is going on at the unconscious level. People obviously don't wake up in the morning and say 'Hmm, I think I'll start the day by focusing on visual information; and then after the coffee break I'll switch over to auditory information'.)

We've already talked about making mental maps, and how

they are likely to vary from person to person, even when they apparently relate to the same event. But if we are using all of our senses all of the time when we are awake (and quite a lot of the time when we are asleep), why should our mental maps be so varied from one person to the next? Why are we sometimes keenly aware of everything going on around us, and other times we can't see something that's right in front of us?

But if this is an accurate depiction of how we think, *how* do we know which rep' system to pay most attention to? The answer, as far as NLP is concerned, is 'context'.

The term 'context' means 'whatever is going on at the time, as perceived by each individual', which rather importantly is why several people can be together in what seems, to an observer, to be the *same* situation, yet each person has their own unique internal perception of that context.

It is also important to understand that a person's perception of a context can sometimes change quite rapidly. NLP co-creator John Grinder has suggested that we can expect that someone's focus on their rep' systems – based on their perception of the context – may shift as often as every 20–30 seconds.

Even the mention of a particular word in a conversation can alter the context for some people – if the word is connected (*anchored*) to some emotionally charged memory – whilst having no effect at all on someone else in the same conversation for whom the word has no special associations.

Horses for courses

In their book *Frogs into Princes* (1979), Bandler and Grinder described the ways we use our sensory systems, including:

- The *lead system*;
- The *representational system*; and
- The *eye accessing cues*.

These processes are all based on using the same basic sensory systems, though the focus of our awareness and the process involved may be somewhat different in each context.

The lead Ssystem

Our *lead* system is the one we most notice when collecting information from the external world and is determined by the kind of information we want to collect.

Like everything else our lead system may shift depending on context. If, during a conversation (in *auditory* mode), we think we can smell smoke, we may redirect our attention so completely onto our sense of smell (*olfactory* mode), that we lose track of what the other person is saying.

Representational systems

The link between our *lead* system and our *representational* system – the system we pay most attention to when *processing* incoming information – is pretty straightforward. If you were most aware of auditory data when collecting information then it is very likely that you will also process it in auditory model. But again this is dependent on the context. As demonstrated above, a change in the context may cause a major shift in focus.

Sensory predicates

For each of the rep' systems there are numerous *sensory predicates* that can be useful indicators of where someone is focusing their attention. A predicate is a word that implies something else. (In all of the examples below the predicates are the words in italics. The first three examples clearly imply that I am visually focused.)

Someone in 'visual mode' may use phrases like: 'I *see* what you mean', '*Looks* good to me', and '*Show* me more'.
In 'auditory mode' a person might use phrases like: 'I *hear* what you *say*', '*Sounds* good to me', and '*Tell* me more'.
And in 'kinaesthetic mode' I might indicate where my attention is focused by using phrases like: 'I *get* what you're saying', 'I *feel* good about that' or '*Fill me in* on the details'.

The skilful use of sensory predicates is particularly influential because we are usually wholly unaware that this filtering process is taking place. If a conversation between two people is based on different rep' systems they may find effective communication very difficult without knowing why, to the point where they might as well be talking different languages. 'I just couldn't seem to get through to him (or her)'.

Each can hear what the other person is *saying*, without any understanding of what that person *means*:

When Rep' Systems Collide:
Jim: Have you looked at those papers I showed you?
Ann: I'm afraid I was tied up with other business all day.
Jim: You mean you didn't even glance at them?!
Ann: You didn't tell me they had to be dealt with in a hurry.
Jim: Well they do! So when do I see some action?

A 'Shared View':
Sue: Have you looked at those papers I showed you?
Tom: Not yet. You must have seen how busy I've been today.

Sue: So you haven't had a chance to glance through them?
Tom: No I haven't – but now that my desk is clear I'll give them my full attention.
Sue: Great! When will I see your report on my desk?

What's in a mode

By the way, it is important to understand that the various sensory 'modes'/representational systems are aspects of our behaviour. They are definitely *not* 'who we are'. So whilst it is tempting to talk about 'visuals', 'auditories', etc, this can create the mistaken belief that people have just one or two preferred rep' systems which they use all the time. If this were true, once we knew a person's rep' system you could use that same style whenever you communicated with them, in order to be in tune with the way they register what is going on in the world around them. In practice the correct way to do this is to track and match a person's predicates *throughout* an interaction.

Checkpoint actions

Listen out for rep' system predicates being used by the people around you, and notice those you use yourself. How often do you quite naturally match other people's predicates?

One sensory system at a time, practise noticing and matching other people's predicates. Watch out for the effects this has on your communications and how other people respond to you.

Caution: As with all NLP-related 'pacing' techniques, match people's predicates in a subtle and respectful manner.

6

Eye accessing cues

What to watch for

The eye accessing cues are based on first hand observations.
What Bandler and Grinder noticed was that people tend to look
one way or another, moment by moment, depending on which
sensory system they are using and whether they are
remembering something or constructing an image.

> **Note:** *All* of the eye movement diagrams show what
> will be seen by an observer.

Visual cues

The three visual eye positions are:

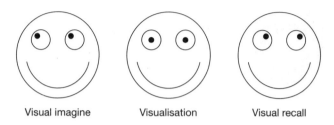

Visual imagine   Visualisation   Visual recall

Whilst images and visualisation are usually associated with seeing, this is not always the case. Visualisation is simply experiencing something in one's imagination. The images can be ongoing or static, and associated or dissociated.

Auditory cues

Auditory mode also has three eye positions:

Auditory imagine   Internal dialogue   Auditory recall

Internal dialogue can be 'self talk' or deciding what you are going to say aloud to someone else. If you watch TV interviews with any kind of spokesperson you will often see them glancing down and to the right (your right), especially if they are asked a question on a particularly sensitive subject.

Kinaesthetic cue

Kinaesthetic mode has only one eye position:

Kinaesthetic recall

This is because you cannot 'construct' a kinaesthetic event without actually experiencing it, which requires recall.

Eye accessing cues seldom occur for more than a short while – in some cases literally as briefly as the blink of an eye. And they always occur in clusters – 'strategies' as they are usually known, which is the main reason for their value. By accurately tracking a person's eye movements, in context you can find out what 'train of thought' they tend to use when reaching a decision, planning some activity and so on.

Strategies

The important difference between identifying rep' systems and identifying strategies is that in the first case one should 'track and match' individual predicates in order to create and/or enhance rapport. Allowing that they will usually occur in matching clusters (again the predicates are in italics):

> **Visual:** I don't *see* what all the fuss is about – it *looks* pretty *clear* to me.
> **Auditory:** It *sounds* like a lot of fuss about nothing, if you *ask* me. I'd *say* it was pretty straightforward.
> **Kinaesthetic:** I don't know why people are *getting* so *upset*. I *found* it pretty straightforward.

Detecting strategies, on the other hand, makes it possible to be more persuasive by verbally matching a complete sequence of eye movements (this does *not* refer to moving your own eyes, as some critics have mistakenly suggested.) So you could find out what qualities someone looks for in, say, a new car, just by asking them. But a conscious answer may not be accurate. So let's track the eye accessing cues instead:

> **Salesperson:** Good afternoon sir.
> **Customer:** Good afternoon. I'm looking for a new family car.
> **Salesperson:** And did you have anything particular in mind?
> **Potential Customer:** I'm not really sure. What do you have?
> **Salesman:** Well we have quite a range of options – a large saloon, an estate, or maybe a people carrier? I wonder, can you give me some idea what features would be important to you?

(In order to answer this question the customer must 'go inside' and think about the features he is being asked about.)

For this example let's suppose that the customer's strategy, as shown in his eye movements, goes:

$$Vc \longrightarrow Ar \longrightarrow Ac \longrightarrow K \longrightarrow K \longrightarrow Vr \longrightarrow K$$

Where:

Ac = auditory image imagined (constructed)
Ar = auditory image remembered
K = kinaesthic image experienced
Vc = visual image imagined, and
Vr = visual image remembered

Whilst these eye movements are going on the customer says:

> **Customer:** Er, yes, I have a rough picture in my mind of the sort of vehicle I'm after.

(The salesperson now has two important clues – their strategy, and the feature which is likely to be most important when it comes to decision time.

This isn't mind reading. The salesperson cannot, and doesn't need to know what the customer is thinking. He needs to verbally replicate the sequence, not the *thoughts*. (The importance of focusing on the *process* rather than on the *content* applies to nearly all NLP-related techniques.)

So now the salesperson uses the sequence to format their own statement.)

> **Salesperson:** So, have you decided what kind of vehicle will meet your requirements?
> (Covert persuasion might shorten the buying process, but it is also likely to cause resistance or even 'buyer's remorse'.)
> **Customer:** I was thinking perhaps one of those people carriers. We do have three children. And a dog.
> **Salesperson** (pointing to a nearby people carrier): I wonder if you can see yourself (Vc) sitting at the wheel of this model? I don't know how your present car sounds (Ar), but this model is very quiet for its size (Ac). Add in the comfort of the seating and the smooth suspension (K) and I promise you'll really enjoy driving (K) this car, even on long journeys. This is probably the best looking vehicle of its kind (Vr – the customer must make a comparison with other cars). And I think you'll be really satisfied (K) with it.

This verbally matches the sequence of eye movements that the customer used as he was deciding what was important to him in a family car, at *this* point in time, in *this* context.

These last two points are crucial. If the customer took some advertising material away to read and came back the next day it could be a big mistake to merely repeat the same sequence. 'Tomorrow,' as Scarlett observed, 'is another day', and eye movement sequences always apply here and now, but not necessarily at any other time. Tomorrow the salesperson would need to evoke a new sequence of eye movements, which might *or might not* be the same as today.

Checkpoint actions

Listen out for the rep' system predicates used by the people around you, and by yourself. How often do you automatically match other people's predicates?

Taking it one sensory system at a time, notice the effects of matching other people's predicates on your communications and how other people respond to you. Caution: As with all NLP-related 'pacing' techniques, match people's predicates in a subtle and respectful manner.

7

Be prepared

States

In NLP, your state at any given time reflects the combination of your emotions, your thoughts and your physiology. You can be in a resourceful state or an unresourceful state; an associated state or a dissociated state; and more precisely, a confident state, a calm state, an agitated state, and so on and so on, which in turn generate particular forms of behaviour.

Moreover, in large measure we create our own states, though we may not necessarily be aware that we are doing it. Thus your physiological state can have a strong influence over your emotional state, and vice versa. If you are in a resourceful state and feeling empowered you are most likely to be taking an upright stance, whether you're standing, sitting or walking, with your head help up and your shoulders pulled back. If, on the other hand, you adopt a pose associated with being down in the dumps – head down, shoulders hunched, etc – then you will be more likely to avoid looking directly at other people, more likely to mumble when speaking to other people and you will probably begin to feel tired or apathetic, dissociated from other people and increasingly introverted for as long as you continue in that kind of pose.

But you have a choice about what state you are in.

For example, if you were about to deliver a presentation wouldn't it be useful to be able to summon up a state of confidence? If you were feeling stressed, wouldn't it be useful to change that into a state of relaxation?

In the past the most common recipe for getting into a certain state tended to be a 'what' statement rather than a 'how' statement. Something like, 'If you want to be confident, think confident.'

How to create a state

But how do you set about doing that?

In this chapter we'll look at two common methods, both of which make use of a technique called anchoring.

Creating anchors

An 'anchor', in NLP, is something which stimulates a complete 'state' response. It may seem a bit clinical that we're talking about things like hearing a piece of music (such as 'our tune') and remembering the sights, sounds and feelings of a very special time spent with a very special person; the smell of a night-flowering plant which brings back a detailed memory of a relaxed evening during a really enjoyable holiday.

Any of the senses, alone or in combination, can be used to create a deliberate anchor, though when teaching someone to create their own anchor(s), some kind of touch seems to be particularly popular. That is to say, to evoke the required state the subject touches themselves in a way they wouldn't do usually (stop sniggering – the idea is to set an anchor which will only be triggered on purpose).

Anchoring a previous experience

The first method involves anchoring a previous, relevant experience. For many people who drive, remembering the moment when they were told that they had passed their driving test is a strong example of a 'confident state'. The anchoring process, then, is as follows:

1. Select a past event when you strongly experienced the state you want to anchor and for which you can recall the sights, sounds and feelings – plus tastes and/or smells, if possible.
2. Recall this experience, preferably as a 'movie' which builds up to the moment when the state was at it's strongest, in as much detail as possible – as long as that doesn't interfere with the flow of the memory.
3. As you sense that the state memory is reaching its peak, create the anchor – touch yourself behind one ear or wherever you want the anchor to be.
4. Hold the anchor until immediately after the state memory passes its peak (this should be no more than about 4-5 seconds).
5. Release your anchor (remove your finger. You're sniggering again!).
6. Repeat steps 3-5, based on the same memory four or five times.
7. Test the anchor by using it without any preliminary recall.
8. If the anchor works, if you successfully experience the state you require, that's it. Otherwise go back to step 2.

Building a state

In the second method you use the same process, but this time applied to an imagined state rather than to the memory of a previous experience.

Once again we start with the three main rep' systems – sight, sound and feeling, and relate them to the state you want to achieve. Initially you can do this by thinking of someone else you actually know of whom you can visualise being in the required state, or you can imagine an imaginary person and what it would be like, for them to be in this state.

Once you have the basic image, including how things look, sound and feel for this other person when they are in the required state, think only about the sensory information and start to associate that with yourself. The important thing is to be as aware as possible of your own reactions as you associate into the state. 'I can see ...', 'I can hear ...', 'I feel ...' rather than 'It would be like I was seeing ...' or 'I think I'd see...'.

Again I realise that this may seem strange to anyone who has not come across these ideas before, but I assure you they are based on what are now well-known scientific principles.

It has almost become a cliché to say that the brain cannot tell the difference between genuine memories and fake memories, but it is nevertheless true. According to the findings of researchers such as Professor Elizabeth Loftus, we actually tend to edit our memories (ie the information that makes up a memory) every time we retrieve them. Indeed, Professor Loftus carried out experiments which showed that around 30 per cent of the subjects automatically incorporated fictional accounts of childhood events – such as visiting Disneyland or getting lost in a shopping mall – simply as a result of hearing a short description of such an event.

What we are doing by creating a virtual state and then applying it to ourselves is simply a deliberate utilisation of a skill most people are already using. We are literally creating a memory and then, using the anchoring technique (as described on the previous page), re-enforcing the power of that new 'memory'.

Qualifications

Just two last points need to be made before we move on:

Be careful what you wish for

Changing your state can be a very useful skill, but the techniques are very powerful and should be used with care. For example, you have to do a presentation, you feel nervous and unsure – a clear example of a situation where you need to summon up a confident state. Right? Possibly, but not if you aren't properly prepared in a way that would justify being filled with confidence. The kind of thing you really want to avoid is striding confidently into the presentation venue and finding that you've forgotten your script, or you don't have the faintest idea how to use the projector.

Richard Bandler, addressing this topic in his book *Using Your Brain For A Change*, recommends creating a state of *competence*, in advance of the event, rather than a state of *confidence* which could easily topple over into *over*confidence.

Be ecological

As an extension of that first point, and in relation to any kind of personal change, always be sure to check the ecology before you start the change process. Remember to set up a pre-change checkpoint – what were you seeing, hearing, and feeling *before* you carried out the change. In particular, be aware of exactly what it is you plan to change, and what there is that is distinctive about your initial state that will tell you when you have returned to it if the change doesn't work out for whatever reason.

Checkpoint action

It is a good idea to practice 'anchoring' purely for the purpose of becoming competent. Do think carefully about where you place such anchors, however. Be sure to leave plenty of places where you can conveniently create any anchors you are actually going to use.

8

Know what you want to get what you want

What do you *really* really want?

As indicated in the last chapter, the results we get in life are largely self-generated. That is to say, we tend to notice the things that confirm our current expectations. In order to succeed you must assume and believe that you are going to succeed. But this is more than mere 'positive thinking'.

> **Whether you think you will succeed or you think you will fail, it is almost certain that you will be proved correct.**

But how will you recognise success? Motivational speakers and pep rallies actually have a strictly limited, short-term effect. Consider this example of a sales director intending to inspire his 'troops':

You are the greatest sales team it has ever been my privilege to lead. In the coming year we must be leaner and fitter, make more sales and maximise our profits. The recent downturn may be over but we aren't out of the woods yet.

We *can* do it. I *believe* we can do it. I *know* we can do it!

Like the proverbial company mission statement the rhetoric is stirring, but what does it really mean? What is the measure of 'leaner and fitter'? How many extra sales equal 'more'? Does this mean that the sales people will no longer be able to offer ad hoc discounts to special customers, for example?

Pareto's Law suggests that 20 per cent of a company's customers will account for approximately 80 per cent of its sales. But does the sales manager want his team to 'maximise profitability' by ignoring the less profitable 80 per cent of their customer base?

The audience may give the sales director a standing ovation as he finishes his speech, but will anyone actually improve their performance as a result of this purely emotive appeal?

Almost certainly 'no', mainly because there are no specific outcomes to which the sales people can respond.

The power of a well-formed outcome

Defining outcomes is a process of self-empowerment.

If I have a well-formed (clearly defined) outcome, I can make effective decisions about what I am prepared to do in order to achieve that outcome. I will also be able to assess whether, at any stage, my outcome has become impractical and must be adapted or abandoned.

Without a well-formed outcome I have little choice but to simply react to what is going on around me. Without a clear sense of direction, regardless of my status, I will be relatively ineffectual. As a result, I am likely to become increasingly frustrated, resentful and possibly even vindictive.

People respond to and work well for a person who obviously knows what they are doing, and is able to communicate positively and effectively with superiors, colleagues and subordinates. How are you going to convince anyone that you know what you are doing, let alone encourage them to follow your lead, if your outcome(s) aren't clear to you?

> **Your perceptions and thoughts are interactive, therefore your current outcome will help to decide which external and internal signals you are consciously aware of.**

What does success look, sound and feel like?

Let's suppose your foremost ambition is to become wealthy. Wealth itself is relative, of course, so merely expressing your desires in a phrase such as 'I want to be wealthy' really isn't saying much at all. Is that wealthy as compared to someone living on the street, as compared to your current situation, or as compared to someone who is 'financially independent' (another pretty vague description)?

If we turn that vague want into a 'well-formed outcome' it becomes far more focused, and therefore far more achievable.

I want to be wealthy, and I'll know I am wealthy when:

- **I hear people talking about my beautiful country home, my smart clothes and my top of the range sports car.**
- **I see that my bank balance always exceeds £1 million.**
- **I feel relaxed, comfortable and unpressured at all times.**

Notice that an outcome is *always* expressed in positive statements. 'I don't want to be poor' or 'I never want to have to work again' may accurately describe your viewpoint, but they leave you facing an *undesirable* state and away from the *desired* state. 'I'll know I am wealthy when...' implies a positive progression, a sequence of improvements leading to the achievement of the desired state.

In the earlier example, the sales director would be likely to achieve more lasting results if he set more precise targets:

> This time next year I want to be able to announce that our sales for the year went over the £17 million mark. I want to see every one of you better your year-on-year figures by at least 15 per cent.
>
> I feel proud to be at the head of such a professional team. Together we *can* do it. I *believe* we can do it. I *know* we can do it!

To fume, or not to fume

As we saw in Chapter 1, our emotional reactions are actually based on our *perceptions* of the events we encounter. Let's apply that knowledge to a practical situation.

Imagine that you are the production manager of a light engineering company which makes, amongst other things, oven doors for a leading manufacturer of kitchen appliances. How might you react to the following events?

- **You arrive at the office and one supervisor reports that production in his department will stop before the end of the shift because they are running out of handles.**
- **The supervisor in the press shop reports reduced output because there were six absentees on the night shift, and they are also running short of the metal 'blanks' which are made into handles.**

- The stock controller says he has ordered more sheet
  metal but the supplier reports several drivers are off
  sick and they can't deliver in less than two to three
  days.

So, what would *you* do?

You could get very angry, shout and curse at your own people
and then phone up the suppliers and threaten to sue them for
breach of contract if they don't deliver the ordered material by
the end of the day. If you set this down as an outcome it would
presumably look something like this.

I want to:

- see everyone rushing around like a load of bluebottles
  in a jam jar, trying to make something out of nothing;
- hear lots of excuses and arguments and later on have
  the MD asking why customers aren't getting their
  deliveries in time;
- feel totally frustrated and get a sore throat from
  shouting at everyone.

Taking control

An alternative outcome might go like this.

I want to:

- see the production line running to schedule and goods
  going out of the door on time;
- hear the supervisors telling me that everything is
  running smoothly, and the sales department telling me
  the customer has placed new orders because they are so
  pleased with the quality of the work and the prompt
  deliveries;

- **feel calm and in control. I am able to respond appropriately and creatively in any crisis.**

With this attitude you can identify the key requirement in this situation – to get hold of some raw stock to feed the presses so that the production line can keep going. With a little thought you come up with a suitable solution. For example, you telephone your suppliers and confirm that the sheet metal is ready to be delivered. Then you call up a local haulier and arrange for a lorry to fetch the material as soon as possible.

Being realistic, maybe the raw materials still won't arrive in time to keep the production line running till the end of the day, but it'll be back on stream tomorrow. You may have to pay some overtime to have a lorry unloaded outside normal hours. And maybe you'll have to contact a staff agency to get a full quota of operators in the press shop tonight.

Yet even with all these drawbacks you'll still be better off than if you simply stomp around venting your anger on everyone in sight.

Impressive results

A number of goal-setting acronyms have been used in the business world at one time or another – such as **SMART**, **S**pecific, **M**easurable, **A**chievable, **R**ealistic and **T**imely. Since NLP addresses the task of setting 'well-formed outcomes', it also defines specific requirements for that process. Strangely enough, however, there is no single acronym for the NLP process. So here's one I prepared earlier:

Individual. As far as possible, your goals should be things that you can achieve more or less by your own efforts. The more your goals rely on other people's actions, agreement, co-operation, etc, the more chances there are for you to lose control of the process and end up with results which, at best, only approximate to your intended outcome.

Measurable. You need to define, in advance, the criteria you will use to determine when you have achieved your goal. These measures both act as a way of gauging, at any moment, whether your task is complete and also help you to ensure that you are 'progressing' in the right direction.

Positive. In order to stay focused on achieving your goal you need to have some kind of representation of the goal inside your head – a mental map, in fact. And, since you cannot make a mental map of a negative, it must be created in the positive in order to be effective.

Realistic. Bearing in mind the time and resources available to you, what can you realistically hope to achieve? Sometimes this part of goal setting can be very frustrating because you begin to realise that the goal you wanted to aim for isn't realistic. To resolve the problem and avoid that frustration, simply break your overall goal down into smaller chunks (see Chapter 15) – a series of lesser goals, each of which is realistic in its own right, and each of which contributes to the realisation of that greater goal.

Ecological. Imagine that you have already achieved your goal. How does everything around you look, sound and feel? Whilst you have successfully achieved your goal, have you discovered any 'downside' to the situation? Is there anything you can alter about the way you achieved your goal that would improve the situation? Are there any other people or plans you forgot to take into consideration? And even if things are OK in the short term, can you detect any way in which achieving your current goal might interfere with your strategic or long-term goals?

Specific. The more specific your goal the easier it will be to determine what you need to do to attain that goal, and whether you are staying on track to achieve your intended outcome. This in turn makes it far more likely that you will reach a satisfactory conclusion. Most of us have wished we were rich, at one time or another, and maybe we dreamed about what it would be like – a 'nice' house, a 'brand new' car, holidays at 'exotic' locations, etc. And how many of us have realised those dreams? Not many.

It is said that when film star Jim Carrey started acting he wrote himself a cheque for $10 million. He kept the cheque in his wallet and, whenever things weren't going too well, he took the cheque out, looked at it and put it away again. Until the day came when he signed a contract giving him $10 million for a single film. On that day he took the cheque out, tore it up and threw it away.

Sustainable. And finally, unless your goal is purely short-term, make sure you have a real chance of keeping your plan going in the long term as well. Far too many new businesses start up and then fail within a matter of a year or two, or even less, because the would-be entrepreneur(s) considered what was necessary to get a cherished project up and running, but gave little or no thought as to how they were going to manage it on a day-to-day basis.

Checking off any new plan or project against a list like this cannot *guarantee* success, of course, but it gives us a far better chance of anticipating potential trouble spots than if we simply launch into a new project, feet first, with not even a hint of a proverbial 'Plan B' waiting in the background.

Checkpoint actions

1. Again, listen to conversations between people at work, but this time aim to detect each person's PTS.
2. Once you think that you have identified someone's PTS, see what happens if you match that PTS – and then deliberately shift into a different PTS. (Only do this with someone who won't take offence if they spot what you are doing.)
3. Is there a specific state of mind – calmness, confidence, creativity or whatever – which you would like to be able to access at will?

- Think back to a time when you were in that state.
- Take note of your feelings (emotional and physical), what you heard and saw and even anything you smelt or tasted.
- Make your mental pictures as large, bright and focused as possible, make the sounds clear and audible, let your posture reflect what you are feeling, and so on. This must be done in an 'associated' state. (In NLP all personal experiences are identified as 'associated' (you are involved in the event), or 'dissociated' (you are watching the event as an outside observer).)
- As the experience becomes really strong, touch yourself briefly but firmly behind your left ear lobe with your left forefinger.
- Repeat the process several times, and then test the link by repeating the physical gesture whilst thinking about something quite different.
- Repeat the entire cycle until the physical gesture immediately calls up the positive memories. (This may take several attempts when you first try it, but you will find that the results are well worth the effort.)

9

Building relationships

The vital link

It is commonly accepted that the success of *any* person-to-person communication depends on the extent to which rapport exists between the people involved. And generally speaking, when we talk about rapport we mean things like trust, harmony, etc. In NLP terms, however, these things are the *consequence* of establishing rapport – they are not themselves rapport. From the NLP perspective, rapport is the process of establishing and maintaining contact with a person at a *non*-conscious level.

The value of making contact at a non-conscious level is that it bypasses the various, often very arbitrary, filters we exercise at the conscious level. It must be said, however, that this is something of a two-edged sword (it cuts both ways!).

The business process re-engineering (BPR) movement of the 1990s used jargon that spoke the language of efficiency to the captains of industry, whilst simultaneously whispering threats of mass redundancy to the troops.

Even when things are going well, as Sue Knight explains in

her book *NLP at Work*: 'Most business decisions are made on the basis of rapport rather than technical merit.' This fact was neatly illustrated in an article in *Computing* magazine which dealt with the selection of IT training:

> As many as 91% of respondents said suppliers were selected by word of mouth, rather than a structured evaluation based on supplier presentations...

I am not a number...

Rapport isn't only important at the person-to-person level. When a company exceeds a certain size, or is distributed over a number of separate sites, effective centralised management becomes nigh on impossible and internal cohesiveness begins to suffer.

Without rapport, management style tends to become either inflexible and bureaucratic, or fragmented and vague. In either case the company will reflect the negative effects in its overall performance, yet it seems that there are still plenty of companies which clearly do not understand the significance of rapport.

It is a basic tenet of NLP that the language we use will both reflect and shape the way we think about the world around us.

Take a look at the short list of terms below and see which column you think is more likely to promote rapport:

A	B
HR (Human Resources)	People
HRD (Human Resource Development)	Training/Education
O&R (Organisation and Resources)	Personnel Department

I am a free man!

NLP is about *increasing* people's effectiveness and *maximising* their potential. Moreover, unlike some recent developments in the business world, NLP achieves its results by fostering constructive individuality, in a constructive manner.

The emphasis in BPR was on tighter controls, downsizing, cost-cutting exercises, and so on, with little or no thought for the role of the individual within the organisation. Yet despite all the hype, BPR failed to deliver the goods.

Why? Because BPR is about theories, not people. James Champy, co-author of *Re-engineering the Corporation* wrote:

> ... within the past five years we have trained a generation of managers who believe that a company is developed by reducing costs. If re-engineering only takes a cost focus, there's a high risk that it will reduce the capability and capacity of the organization. People can't survive in companies that are shrinking.

As the degree of rapport in the work environment goes down, so the work itself quickly seems to lose its intrinsic value and employees become increasingly alienated. As one professional told me, as though it was patently obvious: 'Work is what you do to make the money to do what you really want to do.'

Turning the tide

Rapport is the antidote to all of these negative factors. At an individual level it allows us to create more effective personal relationships, easily and quickly, even with complete strangers.

At a company level rapport provides a basis for effective empowerment and optimal working relationships between staff and management, between departments, and so on.

Rapport can also improve customer relations – if you take the trouble to show people that you respect their beliefs and values. YOU DO NOT have to share those values and beliefs, only acknowledge them in a positive manner.

Karen Boylston, a director of the Centre for Creative Leadership, confirms the fact that this is a key business issue:

> Customers are telling businesses, 'I don't care if every member of your staff graduated with honours from Harvard, Stanford and Wharton [top US business colleges]. I will take my business and go where I am understood and treated with respect.'

Another aspect of rapport, then, is the ability to show someone that you 'understand and respect them as a human being'.

The time and the place

It is worth saying that the best relationships come about when we use rapport to create interaction at an *appropriate* level.

In a family context it would be appropriate to develop a deep rapport. In a romantic relationship the level of rapport might run to passionate. In a business context, however, a feeling of mutual respect is usually quite sufficient.

The level of rapport we create with each person or group must therefore suit the context. If we work too hard at creating rapport we may lead the other party to imagine that there is more to the relationship than we want or intend.

Going one step further, in a negotiating situation for example, it is a good idea to gently break rapport before making any important decisions to give yourself a chance to judge the current position on its business merits rather than reaching agreement because you don't want to disturb the warmth that has built up between the parties to the negotiation.

A two-way street?

As I said earlier, connecting with someone at a non-conscious level *can* be a two-edged sword for the other person. And here's the reason why.

The phenomenon known as 'buyer's remorse' occurs when we make a decision that is overly influenced by rapport. Some salespeople aim to deepen the rapport they have with the customer as they go for the 'close'. But it is distinctly one-way rapport – the salesperson is communicating with the customer's unconscious, simply in order to make the sale. As a consequence there is real danger that the customer will regret the purchase – and may come to believe that the salesperson has betrayed them. Not much of a basis for any future dealings!

This is also very relevant in training situations, an important area for many companies, where trainers and clients alike seem to regard very high post-course trainer evaluation as highly desirable. In fact, studies have shown that the higher scoring trainers (81 per cent and over) are quite possibly being scored on their social skills – rather than on the effectiveness of their training skills. Trainers who score 61–80 per cent may be creating a less intense, but more appropriate, degree of rapport, and delivering more effective training as measured by results three, six or nine months down the line.

Checkpoint action

In the next two chapters we will be looking at some specific techniques for developing rapport.
For the moment you might like to simply watch how people around you relate to each other and see if you can spot any behaviour patterns which are common to:

a.   **situations with a medium to high level of rapport;**
b.   **situations where rapport is low or even non-existent.**

10

Talking body language

Matching and mirroring

So how do we create rapport? Amongst the NLP techniques that can be used to create rapport are *matching and mirroring* (the other person's behaviour).

The technique is called 'matching and mirroring' because you set yourself up as a 'mirror' for the other person by matching that person's behaviour, directly or indirectly, to varying degrees.

When dealing with groups you will need to match and mirror whoever you are currently speaking to, whilst also paying attention to the person you most wish to influence.

The four mirroring techniques are:

- mirroring *voice tone/tempo*;
- mirroring *breathing rate*;
- mirroring *movement*;
- mirroring *body posture*.

These stratagems are particularly effective:

- **either as a means of creating rapport when some degree of trust has already been established, or**
- **deepening an existing level of rapport.**

Tone and tempo

In a business context, mirroring voice tone and/or speech tempo is probably the most effective way to establish rapport.

It is relatively difficult to spot since few of us have a very accurate idea of what our own voice sounds like to other people. We are even less aware of how our voices change in various situations – it depends on what we think of the person we are talking to, our current emotional state, and so on.

The *tone* of voice can be high or low, loud or soft, clear or mumbled, etc, while the *tempo* can be fast or slow, flowing or hesitant, variable or monotonous. You need only mirror the *general* characteristics of a person's voice. You need not, and should not, try to do an 'impression' of their voice such as copying an accent, quirky mispronunciations, etc.

Generally speaking, a person in kinaesthetic mode will tend to speak quite slowly, often with very noticeable pauses and in a deeper than average tone. Someone in auditory mode is more likely to have an even-paced, well-modulated, interesting voice, while being in visual mode is often characterised by rapid, rather high-pitched speech.

A breath of familiarity

Mirroring a person's *breathing rate* is a very effective way of establishing rapport, but it is also the most difficult, especially if the other person is wearing baggy clothing, keeps shifting around or, worse yet, appears to have stopped breathing.

As a rough guide, someone in kinaesthetic mode will usually breathe quite regularly and fully, from the bottom of their lungs. A person in auditory mode will also breathe quite regularly, but from the mid-chest area. Whilst in visual mode, people tend to breathe quite lightly using only the upper chest.

If you can't see any chest movement at all, watch for the rise and fall of their shoulders, or use a slow, shallow breathing pattern yourself and watch for a response.

Something in the way you move

Matching *body movement* and *body posture* are the easiest forms of mirroring, but should be used with great discretion.

In its most literal form, I might mirror your posture, movements and gestures quite directly. If *you* lean back, then *I* will lean back; if *you* cross your legs to the left, I will cross *my* legs to the left, and so on. The only difference is that I will leave a pause before copying you, and my movements will be quite slow and subtle. The danger here is that you will detect what I am doing, at least subconsciously, and end up feeling irritation rather than rapport.

One way to avoid this error is to simulate just some aspects of the other person's posture and gestures, leaving a varying amount of time before responding to a given movement.

Alternatively, you could use the 'crossover mirroring' technique. Rather than directly copying the other person's actions you make reciprocal gestures. So, if you are tapping the desk with your pencil, I might drum on my knee with my fingers *at the same tempo*. If you cross your legs I cross my arms, etc.

Once again, the emphasis is on using smooth, discreet, apparently independent movements to avoid giving away the fact that you are actually reacting to the other person.

(For details of some recent research on the effectiveness of these techniques see the first section, 'Be a mimic', of the online

New Scientist article here: http://www.newscientist.com/
mg19826551.400-eight-ways-to-get-exactly-what-you-want.
html.)

Watch my hands

Body language is also important in that people often make small
but easily discernible movements that effectively 'point out' their
preferred thinking style at a particular moment:

- Rubbing or pointing to the area around the eyes
  suggests a *visual* mode of thinking. This person may
  not '*see* what you're getting at'. Or perhaps she has
  '*spotted* something interesting' in what you just
  said.
      You can enhance your communication by using
  visual phrases: 'Let me show you what I mean', 'Let me
  clarify that idea', 'Let's put that under the microscope',
  and so on.
- Any noticeable movement around the ears or the mouth
  indicates that *auditory* processing is at work. If someone
  starts pulling at their earlobe, for example, this may
  indicate that they don't 'like what they *hear*', or they
  may be thinking 'there's a lot in what you say'. You
  might respond with phrases like: 'Let me tell you what I
  mean' or 'Let's send a clear message.'
- Gestures with the arms and/or hands usually
  accompany a *kinaesthetic* response. That person may '*feel*
  that some point needs *fleshing out*', or he may
  think that your ideas have given him 'something to get
  to *grips* with'. In which case use lines such as: 'Let's
  kick this idea around', 'lets get to grips with this
  situation' and 'I know you'll feel really comfortable
  with this.'

In each case it is important to note what responses you are getting. These signals are *indicators*, not rules, so it is important to watch for responsive signals such as smiles, head nods and so on.

11

Follow the leader

Walk this way

As long as you are interacting with another person, whether individually or in a group, you will be either pacing or leading that other person. That is to say, regardless of how much or how little you know about NLP, you will either:

- **behave in a way that is similar to the other person's behaviour (in NLP this is called *pacing*), or**
- **behave in a way that is quite unlike the other person's behaviour (known as *leading*).**

Successful *pacing* goes beyond the matching and mirroring techniques described in Chapter 8. To pace someone really effectively you may also need to detect and mirror their beliefs, values and the content of what they say. (However, you don't have to share those beliefs and values in order to mirror them.) Once your pacing creates a sufficient degree of rapport, you can then move on to start leading the person or people you have been pacing. Thus, you can begin to guide the person you are dealing with rather than being led by them and use leading to determine the effectiveness of your pacing.

When pacing – creating rapport – is effective we are communicating with the other person/people in the interaction at a level below their conscious attention. At this level they will normally be more responsive, as long as we do not try to act against them in any way. We can test whether we have actually created that responsive state by *initiating* action instead of following the other person's lead. For example, if we are both sitting with our legs crossed, then instead of waiting for you to make a move I will uncross my legs and straighten up in my seat. If I have indeed created rapport then shortly after I make these moves you will make similar moves. If you don't respond that simply means that we aren't yet in strong rapport, and I need to carry on pacing you for a little longer before I make another 'leading move'.

The fear of flying

Some time ago David (a friend of mine who often uses various NLP techniques) was waiting at an airport with a business colleague who had never flown before and was getting increasingly nervous. David decided that this was a situation which could be resolved by pacing and leading.

Initially, then, David created rapport by getting his colleague to talk about his favourite hobby, with David acting as an ideal audience. Only when the time approached for them to board the plane did David do a little leading (changing his body posture) just to establish that the necessary degree of rapport had been established. Having evoked a positive result, he then went back to pacing the other person until the announcement asking for passengers on their flight to go to the boarding gate. At this point David literally resumed his leading behaviour, gathering up his things and moving to the gate without saying anything about what was happening.

So successful was David in creating rapport that the two men boarded the plane, flew from Gatwick to Edinburgh – 1½ hours, approx – all the while discussing the colleague's hobby. It was only when they were getting into a taxi that the colleague noticed the completely unfamiliar surroundings and consciously realised he had just completed his first flight.

Leading to win

In a business situation, once rapport has been established the pacer should be able to transfer smoothly into leading mode in order to bring the event to its desired conclusion.

But beware. Pacing and leading are most effective when both leader *and* those being led are headed towards a win/win situation. A 'leader' who works for a result where she wins and they lose is likely to find that the manoeuvre falls apart as the 'victims' recognise the true nature, and consequences, of the transaction.

Checkpoint actions

1. Spend a few days taking conscious note of the speaking patterns of people you talk to – tone, tempo, etc.
2. Spend a few more days noticing people's body language.
3. In situations where it will not cause offence if anyone realises what you are doing, match and mirror people's vocal characteristics and body language (but don't do a direct imitation of the other person).
4. Notice what difference it makes for you when you adopt someone else's style of speaking and/or physical posture.

5. Watch how pacing and leading occur between people in workplace interactions. Is it always the more senior person who does the leading?

6. Use body movements and voice to create rapport, then see what changes you need to make in order to:

    a. lead the other person;

    b. break rapport.

12

Give the dog a new name

The higher the fewer

As we have already discovered, an anchor is a *learned* response, which means that we can create, alter and dissolve anchors, at will, in order to achieve specific results. Unfortunately, we can also, quite unintentionally, create inappropriate anchors. For example, in many companies today, the higher you go up the management ladder, the fewer people you will find who have any great length of service in that company, except those at the very top, perhaps.

It is as though companies have developed such a negative view of the link between loyalty and competence that the only way to get promoted is to leave.

Why do companies act this way? At first sight such behaviour may seem somewhat self-defeating, yet it does prove to make sense if we relate it to the NLP concept of anchoring.

Just as a particular feeling can be anchored to a particular piece of music, so our feelings about a particular person can become anchored to a specific situation, such as seeing that person in the same role day after day, month after month.

When this kind of unconscious, unintentional anchoring occurs, when we label someone by their job title (or their sex, or their skin colour), instead of seeing them as a unique individual, or when we evaluate them according to past performance, instead of according to what they are doing now, they can become anchored (in our thoughts) to a particular response. Once this happens it can take something like a resignation before we can clear the anchors and recognise that person's true worth.

Companies with a clear pattern of 'promotion through resignation' need to look very closely at the company culture. Some training in basic people skills may be long overdue.

The same problem exists when we characterise a person by judgemental labels ('maverick', 'loner', etc), as though the person and their behaviour are the same thing. That is to say, when we 'give a dog a bad name'.

Put very simply, we tend to see what we *expect* to see, so when we give someone a label we redraw our mental maps around the label rather than around the person, severely limiting our ability to see beyond the label. Moreover, whilst people cannot change what they 'are', we can change our *behaviour* in any way we want, whenever we want. The biggest barrier to change is usually not in the individual, but in other people's refusal to accept that the person *can* change.

A rose by any other name

We also need to pause here to consider just *how* the way we use words – and especially 'labels' – can heavily influence the way we think about things.

Take the term 'maverick', for example. For one person this may have a negative meaning – someone who is difficult to handle, who is always off doing what *they* want instead of fitting in like a good 'team player'. But is this the meaning that the 'maverick' themself will pick up on? Remember that the title of the autobiography of South America's most famous, and successful, industrialist, Ricardo Semler is: *Maverick!* Indeed, many business books readily acknowledge that a few 'mavericks' are essential to the well-being of any sizeable company precisely because they do routinely challenge the status quo.

So a label intended as a term of disapproval by the person using it may sound like a commendation to the person it is directed at. Result? Instead of discouraging unwanted behaviour, using a label in place of constructive discussion may re-inforce the very behaviour it was meant to deter.

Inadvertent hypnosis

There is now substantial evidence that we all tend to drift in and out of a 'trance state' on a regular basis throughout our waking hours. During these incidents, which occur every 90 minutes and last for some 15–20 minutes (both timings are approximate), we may find that we are clumsier, more easily distracted and more suggestible. This pattern of trances, known as the *ultradian rhythm*, seems to be our intuitive way of taking time to process incoming information.

The existence of these trances shows our ability to go in and out of 'altered states of consciousness' in an easy and natural manner, and helps to explain what I call 'inadvertent hypnosis'.

Suppose, for a moment, that you have the job of helping someone learn to ride a bike. Would you tell them:

'Keep it steady'

or would you say:

'Don't let it wobble.'

Although the difference between these two phrases may seem very trivial, yet in the real world the first instruction will be heard as a positive and supportive command, whilst the second is an invitation to disaster. The point to note is that we often cannot hear *exactly* what is being said.

Don't think about a blue elephant

OK, are you *not* thinking about a blue elephant? Of course you aren't. It just isn't possible to know whether you are *not* thinking about something unless you think about that thing in order to know what it is you're not going to think about!

The human brain simply cannot think in negatives, so if I say 'Don't let it wobble' the listener must first think about wobbling in order to know what it is they shouldn't do – and will probably wobble all over the place in the process. But if I say 'Keep it steady', no such complications arise and the trainee can choose to do precisely that.

Checkpoint actions

1. As you meet with people you know, be aware of the extent to which your reactions are based on past events. Are you really seeing people as they are now, or as they used to be?
2. When decisions have to be made, to what extent do you choose to do things 'the way we've always done them'? Are you losing out on efficiency and creativity by refusing to accept the need for, and likely benefits of, change?

13

When you put it like that

It's the way you tell 'em

Two people say almost exactly the same thing, yet one version sounds like a threat, and one is a simple comment.

Why? Because everything that happens, happens 'in context'. When someone speaks to us we take account of who they are, what we think about them, and so on. If a friend telephones and says 'Have you got a minute?' in a cheery tone of voice, that will have totally different connotations compared with a situation where your boss ambushes you as you pass his office and asks in a sombre tone 'Have you got a minute?'

> **The meaning of what you say is the response that it gets.**

In NLP jargon, everything we say and do occurs within what is referred to as a 'frame'. We've all been in a situation when, for no apparent reason, people responded to us in a way that was totally at odds with our intentions. It's as though they were responding to the frame instead of to the picture.

For example, you might be in a meeting where some future event is being planned and you make what you think is quite obviously a suggestion. One of the other people in the meeting turns on you, however, and criticises you for being so pushy and for not waiting to see what everyone else has to say.

Quite possibly what has happened here is that you have been talking about the event using the 'as if' frame ('as if' the event had actually happened as you described) without making it clear that it was meant to be purely speculative.

What will they hear when you speak?

So, an effective frame is more than just another way of saying something – it must also get your listener(s) to 'see' whatever it is you're talking about in a new way. For example:

> It isn't easy for me to say this, because I know it may sound unpleasant, and it may seem as though I haven't given you credit for all the hard work that you've put into preparing this presentation. It is my job to make sure that we show ourselves to our customers in the best possible light. And because of that I'm going to ask you to go back and rework this presentation.
>
> It needs to be shorter and punchier – not more than 40–45 minutes, maximum – and I want you to replace the jargon with language that the customer will understand.
>
> Is that clear?

This explanation gives what might otherwise seem like naked criticism and frames it in terms of 'what we need to show the customer'. This shows that you've given some thought to how your comments might be perceived.

Notice the use of the word 'because' towards the end of the

first paragraph. Although no one seems to know why, an explanation, even a weak one, often appears far more persuasive if it includes the word 'because'.

The second paragraph – 'It needs...' – offers some constructive guidelines for improvement, and also shows that you've given the matter some thought rather than just reacting.

Lastly, 'Is that clear?' is ambiguous enough to be answered yes or no, or to open the way for more discussion, if necessary.

Requests can also benefit by being well framed, with the *reason* for the request coming *before* the request itself:

> I don't know if you're aware of this fact – a recent internal study showed that it takes a programmer several days to produce a single page for the company website. And even then the result often leaves a lot to be desired.
>
> There's a graphic design package I've been looking at which allows the user to create pages as good as or better than the ones we have in a fraction of the time and in such a way that we could change things like the font, background colour and so on with just a couple of clicks of a mouse button. It can even check the spelling and grammar – and we know from experience how important that can be. It's pretty expensive, but I believe it could pay for itself in a few weeks.
>
> That's why I'm suggesting that we provide each member of the website team with a copy of this program.

Apart from a hint of a request at the start of the third paragraph, it is only after some very relevant advantages have been described that we finally find out what the speaker is actually asking for. The listener cannot reasonably respond to the request until it has been clearly specified – in the final sentence!

But suppose the speaker had started out in reverse order:

> I'm putting in this request to supply the website designers with copies of a graphics design program.
>
> I don't know if you're aware of this fact – a recent internal study showed that it takes a programmer several days...

This way round, the listener can make a decision immediately and totally ignore the explanation, no matter how good.

Sweetening the pill

About 70–80 per cent of the population tend to be resistant to change, to a greater or lesser extent. This means that the way in which news of a change is presented is often crucial to successful implementation of that change. Here again, framing can make the difference between success and failure.

When introducing new technology, for example, salesmen and enthusiasts tend to use phrases like:

- 'It's a whole *new way* of working.'
- 'This will *revolutionise* working practices.'
- 'These are the machines *of the future*.'

Imagine how these phrases must sound to someone who is averse to change. No wonder so many people, including many managers, still show signs of technophobia.

How much easier would it be if the new technology was introduced within a more sensitive frame, such as:

- 'A way to make your job *easier*.'
- 'In most respects, *as straightforward as* using a typewriter.'
- '*Full training* will be provided.'

By changing the phrasing, the changes become *evolutionary* rather than *revolutionary*, and much less threatening.

On the other hand...

Where framing *creates* a context, reframing *reshapes* the context. It is a way of reviewing an existing situation or idea so that the content can be re-evaluated. It can be a very powerful way of expanding someone's understanding of their existing map of a particular situation.

Long-termism versus short-termism in business is just one example of how reframing has become a badly needed skill.

In the world of computer programming, for instance, there has been a trend towards:

- **shedding permanent staff;**
- **making increasing use of contract labour.**

In the short term this has at least two important advantages:

- **Contractors only need be employed as long as there is work for them to do.**
- **Specialist skills can be bought in when needed rather than paying for regular staff to be trained up.**

If we reframe the action, however, we see that there are limitations as well as advantages:

- **Contractors don't have the same loyalty or self-interest in the success of the company as do permanent staff members.**
- **If your systems have been developed by a group of people who have all moved on, who is there in-house who really understands what it's all about?**

The initial frame seemed very attractive, and was correct, as far as it went. Only by reframing the possible outcomes can we appreciate both the advantages and the drawbacks of each alternative, decide whether the action is still worth taking, and, if it is, how we can minimise any negative side effects.

Trouble is a state of mind

By reframing we can alter our perception of a situation and may even find an advantage we had previously overlooked.

One important reframe concerns CRM (customer relationship management). Customer-facing staff may think that customers want everything, yesterday, and preferably for free. And it's true; some customers can be difficult. Then again, without any customers, where's your business?

The reframe here is simple: If all customers can be difficult at some time or other, then having difficulties with customers is part of being in business. Difficult customers aren't a burden at all – they are proof of success!

Checkpoint actions

1. You have to ask someone to re-do a task when there really isn't any excuse for not having done it properly the first time round.
   - How would you frame your comments to get a positive response?
   - How do you feel about trying to be positive when the other person is so clearly at fault?

   Repeat this exercise with several different work colleagues in mind.
   Is there a difference depending on the person you have in mind? If so, why?

2. Make it a habit, whenever you hear a negative comment, to look for a striking reframe. For example:

   Comment: 'I hate getting up at 7.00 am every morning!'
   Reframe: 'You wouldn't have that problem if you didn't have a job – and the salary that goes with it.'

   Do this in response to your own negative thoughts.

14

Meta programs and motivation

'Quick fix' thinking

Years ago, one of the managers I was working with at the time came back from an interpersonal skills workshop and announced that he had made a major discovery: 'You can't motivate other people, and it's a waste of time trying'.

Well, if motivating someone means getting them so fired up that they'll work flat out for the next 50 years with no further intervention then no, you cannot motivate another person.

If, on the other hand, we're talking about understanding what gets someone excited, or turned off, so that we can encourage them to follow or avoid a certain course of action, then we certainly can motivate other people quite effectively. Especially when we understand which meta programs are involved for that person.

Even if we've never heard the term, we all use various *meta programs*. They help us to sort and/or prioritise information. They help us to decide the relative importance, or unimportance, for us, of the events going on around us. And they provide us with a way of streamlining our interactions with our surroundings rather than having to think each situation through 'from scratch'.

The downside of such 'quick fix' thinking is that sometimes the programs take over, which is very often what is happening when we talk about someone showing a 'knee-jerk reaction' to some event.

The upside is that when we know which meta programs people work to in a given situation and how, we can literally 'customise' our communication on a person-by-person basis and interact with other people far more efficiently, thereby leading to all kinds of win/win results.

> **Meta programs, like other ideas in NLP work best when we deal with people as they are – not as we think they should be.**

A new approach

When we recognise which filters someone is using, and how (even though they may not know themselves), we can stop drifting from one 'why on earth did they do that?' experience to another. Instead we can begin to understand the underlying structure or framework within that person's behaviour. And from that we can begin to anticipate how they are likely to react to the things going on around them – including our own input.

Having said that, there are an almost unlimited number of meta programs, and no book can give a complete list. Most authors of introductions to NLP have therefore contented themselves with only a token list of names and descriptions. This time I want to use a new approach, by explaining a process you can use to create any meta program you need.

I will finish the chapter by describing some of the existing meta programs which are especially relevant to the use of NLP in the workplace. Both for information and so that you can get some idea of what 'real life' meta programs look like.

A typical meta program

There are two basic meta program formats – analogue and digital. An analogue meta program is one where there is a continuous range of options. The 'Sameness/Difference' meta program, for example, is analogue in structure, usually set out as:

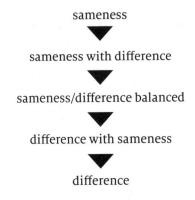

sameness

▼

sameness with difference

▼

sameness/difference balanced

▼

difference with sameness

▼

difference

That is, some people prefer things to be the same (consistent), some people like sameness but with occasional differences, some people like a balance between the two – or are equally at home with sameness or differences – some people prefer difference with some degree of sameness, and some people like a situation where things are regularly changing.

But what does this apply to, you might ask. In essence, like many of the NLP-related techniques, this scale is context-dependent. Some people like plenty of change in the workplace, but want to go home to a haven of sameness at the end of the day, whilst other people might like the frisson of having ongoing change in all areas of their life.

Part of the skill of using the meta programs is being able to elicit this information without having it seem as though you are running an interrogation.

Digital meta programs, on the other hand, are based on a set of fixed options. In the towards/away from meta program, for instance, there are just two important options. Other intermediate options are possible, but in a genuinely digital meta program it will be obvious that any intermediate options are harder to identify, and less important than the main options.

Creating a meta program
Towards/away from – an example

One of the simplest of the NLP-related meta programs is called towards/away from. The focus of the meta program is: when someone has to make a choice in a given context, are they more likely to consider what they want (what they want to move towards), or what they don't want (what they want to avoid or move away from)?

Determining relevance

The first step in creating a meta program is to identify a characteristic which will be important in a given situation. To do this you need to determine the 'meaning' of your meta program.

In the case of the towards/away from pattern we are talking very much about how people motivate themselves and how they can be motivated by others.

This has a very obvious relevance in business. It is useful to know, for example, whether a given employee is more readily motivated by being offered a reward (a bonus payment, for example), or by being offered the opportunity to avoid something (avoid late night working, avoid a poor rating come annual review time, etc).

As well as finding out which meta program(s) are important in a given context, it is also important to know about a person's position on each relevant meta program. Thus the towards/away from pattern is relevant to almost any job. But we also need to know which option an individual is likely to go for in a given situation.

Someone who has a towards attitude will usually be a better team leader, for example, than someone who tends to be away from oriented, because they are more likely to be aiming to succeed, as compared with the away from-oriented person who may spend too much time looking for hypothetical problems. Having said that, it may be an advantage to give someone who tends to be away from-oriented responsibility for keeping everyone else's feet on the ground (roughly the equivalent of Edward de Bono's 'black hat' character).

Determining the range

Having identified the characteristic we next need to determine whether an analogue or a digital scale would be most appropriate. As a very general rule of thumb it is probably best to use an analogue scale unless you are sure that you have two or more clearly discrete (separate) markers.

In the case of the towards/away from meta program, for example, this is almost always presented as an either/or choice, but as James and Woodsmall pointed out in *Time Line Therapy and the Basis of Personality* (Meta Publications, 1988), the two basic options could be expanded upon to include:

- **Towards with a little away from;**
- **Both towards and away from equally;**
- **Away with a little towards.**

Though this is really a judgement call for the person making the assessment. In practise we would only be likely to add the extra categories if we needed a high level of precision. Otherwise the basic either/or choice would be entirely satisfactory.

In another meta program, the Primary Interest Filter, we are specifically asked for a 'first choice' from a list; 'In a given context are you most interested in: People, Place, Things, Activity or Information?' Of course we could still answer something like, 'people and information', only that doesn't provide the answer called for in the question.

It is important, then, to consider, where a genuine choice is available, whether an analogue or digital scale is most appropriate – and to make this choice in relation to the context where the meta program will come into play rather than as a universal generalisation.

Elicitation questions

Having created a meta program, the final step is to create one or more questions which will elicit (draw out) a person's position on a given meta program in a given situation.

Two basic kinds of question are used to elicit this information – 'open' and 'closed'. Closed questions are more like a multiple choice test rather than calling for a simple yes/no. Thus, in the case of the primary interest filter example, we could ask a very straightforward (closed) question such as:

What is most important to you when you go on holiday: is it the people, the place, the architecture and 'stuff', the various activities, or the opportunity to learn about the history and culture of somewhere new?

In the case of the towards/away from meta program and others of that kind, asking an either/or question may seem too blunt, in which case it may be better to ask an open question which allows the subject to answer you in their own fashion. Thus you might ask an open question such as:

What's the most important thing about your job – as far as you're concerned?

This time you may need to do a bit of 'reading between the

lines', noticing whether the answer is more concerned with the benefits of having the job ('They provide really good health and dental coverage', 'I can be with the family every weekend', etc), or what having the job shields them from ('I don't have to worry about anyone in the family getting sick or needing dental work,' 'I'm not expected to do any overtime').

NLP time

Unlike most other meta programs, people tend to be fairly consistent as regards their attitude towards time.

Towards–away from

For motivational purposes a person in towards mode needs to be pointed in the right direction and given their head (with occasional discreet checking to ensure that they stay on course).

A person in away from mode can be motivated by threats, but take care, if the threats become too intense they may become afraid to do anything at all.

Options–procedures

When someone is in options mode they will appreciate having plenty of freedom to make their own choices. Someone in procedures mode, on the other hand, prefers sticking to tried and tested lines of action.

A person in options mode really doesn't need motivating as self-motivation is one of their main strengths; rather they need to be kept firmly (but not too obviously) on track.

A person in procedures mode is best motivated if they are given detailed instructions. They need to make few if any choices, and they can earn praise when they adhere to the standard procedures.

Proactive–reactive

People operating in proactive mode are also self-motivators; the people who are regularly one step ahead of their colleagues. On the downside they will often ignore the analysis and planning which is needed when making important decisions.

People who feel more comfortable in reactive mode are often noted for their love of collecting information and careful planning before doing anything at all. In proactive mode, collecting information is done as part of an overall planning process; in reactive mode it is more likely to be used as a delaying tactic because they'd really rather do nothing at all. That is to say, to avoid commitment and responsibility, not because they are lazy.

Convincer evidence

These are four known ways of collecting/presenting evidence to make it convincing, with the first and second 'channels' being the most frequently used:

- **Visually: the person must be able to literally see the information in order to be convinced (true for about 55 per cent of the population in a business context).**
- **Aurally: the person must be able to hear the evidence, in a presentation, by word-of-mouth recommendation or whatever (applies to about 30 per cent of business people).**
- **Activity: the evidence must be presented in a way that allows 'hands on' experience of the product or service (true for about 12 per cent of the business community).**
- **Reading: the evidence must be delivered in written or printed format so that the person can read it for themselves (true for about 3 per cent of the business population).**

Convincer frequency

Assuming that the information is presented using the appropriate mode, how many times do you need to be shown the evidence in order to be persuaded?

- **Automatic: these people make their minds up in no time flat, often on very little information.**
- **Several times: people in this group need to see the evidence several times, though the precise number (usually less than 10) will depend on the person and the situation.**
- **Consistent: these people are never fully convinced and need regular confirmation that their decision was correct.**
- **Period of time: people in this group need to have things repeated over a given period of time rather than on a specific number of occasions. Here, too, the precise length of time will vary according to the person and the situation.**

Sameness–difference

Look at the pattern below and, as quickly as you can, write down a brief description of how the shapes are related.

Someone in sameness mode would simply notice that all three shapes are the same. To sameness people, the similarity they see in the world around them is more important than the differences, though they may sometimes acknowledge the differences as an afterthought.

Differences people will note the dissimilarities before anything else, while sameness with difference people will start with the similarities and then add on the difference(s) as in the description, 'All three shapes are triangles, but two shapes are pointing upwards, and the middle shape is pointing downwards.'

As far as motivation is concerned, sameness people naturally respond to conformity, traditional standards and ways of doing things, rather than to newness and innovation.

People in difference mode, and the two 'with qualification' groups, are more likely to appreciate 'newness', 'freshness', 'progress' and 'improvement' (try watching TV adverts with this thought in mind!). Those in the unqualified 'difference' group, are often attracted to innovation for its own sake.

Frame of reference (internal–external) filter

This meta program considers how people make judgements about their own actions. If you ask someone: 'How do you know when you've done well at a given task?' they may answer that they go by other people's reactions (eg peer pressure) or that they have some kind of internal yardstick. Or some combination of the two.

1. External reference
2. External reference with internal check
3. Balanced
4. Internal reference with external check
5. Internal reference.

People with a significant element of external reference are quite easily motivated since they interpret approval, or disapproval, as the measure of how well they are performing.

A person with an internal frame of reference is really only focused on his/her own opinions. Where someone in external mode hears even mild input as commands, a person in internal mode hears external input, even direct commands, as mere information. These people may be hard to motivate unless you frame your approach in the appropriate terms.

Modal operators

Modal operators owe much of their power to the fact that they often crop up in people's 'self talk'. A person can learn to be a modal operator in their childhood and go on using it for life, never asking whether it has outlasted its usefulness.

The most frequently encountered operators include:

- **can – can't**
- **could – couldn't**
- **must – must not (mustn't)**
- **need to – don't need to (needn't)**
- **ought – ought not (oughtn't)**
- **possible – impossible**
- **should – shouldn't**
- **will – won't**

The modal operators are not really meta programs, but they work in a similar manner. To use them as motivators listen to how people use them. If you suggest a certain course of action, and the reply comes back: 'I wouldn't think so – it looks impossible', an effective response would be: 'Okay, I can see why you might think it was impossible for some people, but for you I think it looks like it would be possible.'

Corporate meta programs

Meta programs can also be found as the foundations of company culture. These are some extreme examples:

- Procedure mode – very little innovation
- Options mode – just a step away from bankruptcy
- Towards – Overemphasis on personal development
- Away from – primary occupation, 'fire-fighting'.

Checkpoint actions

- Check your own meta programs. Starting with the list given in this chapter, make a quick note of what you guess is your own position on each program – then take a few days to find out what you actually do, in the work context.
- What do the results of this exercise tell you? Remember that once you know what you actually do you have the freedom to change anything you think could be improved on.
- Notice what meta program positions are encouraged in your company. Are there any incongruities – like claiming that innovation is highly valued whilst marginalising anyone who tries to show some initiative? If so, can these incongruities be brought out into the open and dealt with?

15

Making information make sense

Bottom lines and aerial views

You may want to answer the following questions before you read on. It will make the practical application of the information in this chapter much easier to understand.

Q1. When learning about something new, do you prefer to (**A**) start with an overview and work down to specific details, or (**B**) build up to the overall view, starting from the details?

If you chose option **A** then answer **Q2**, otherwise answer **Q3**.

Q2. Are you (**C**) really interested in detailed information, or would you (**D**) prefer to stick with the overview?

Q3. Are you (**E**) really interested in the 'big picture', or would you (**F**) prefer to stick with the details?

Q1	Q2	Q3	Chunk type
A	D	–	Abstract
A	C	–	Abstract to Specific
B	–	F	Specific
B	–	E	Specific to Abstract

Up the down staircase

An important element in Alfred Korzybski's *General Semantics* was what he called the 'ladder of abstraction'. One of the main reasons why we fail to communicate effectively, Korzybski said, was because we so often use *vague* language, and expect other people to understand *precisely* what we mean.

Sometimes this isn't particularly important. If I say that I'm going to London next week, by train, it really doesn't matter whether you understand that I plan to travel first class on the 8.43am Intercity Express from King's Sittingbourne next Friday and will return the same day, or you just think 'London, by train'. But suppose that I want to buy a ticket for that journey – and you are the ticket clerk. In that case it matters a great deal whether you understand exactly what I've planned, because the precise combination of these details will determine what kind of ticket I get and how much it will cost.

The NLP label for the process of moving up or down the ladder of abstraction is *chunking*. When we chunk *up* we start with the details ('specifics') and work up to the overview. Chunking *down* means breaking down an 'abstract' overview into ever more precise details.

In a business context, people who prefer to deal in specifics tend to be 'backroom boys'. They seldom rise very high on the management scale because they don't feel comfortable dealing with 'big picture' thinking, which can seem unnecessarily vague and impractical – which of course it is, since dealing in big chunks takes you into the area of 'what' is to be done rather than 'how' it is to be done.

Those who rise highest on the corporate ladder, even though they may have started out acquiring specific skills, usually have the ability to take in, and make decisions from, the 'big picture' perspective, without getting caught up in the details.

Plus or minus two

According to one famous study, by psychologist George Miller, human beings can only consciously deal with seven 'chunks' of information, plus or minus two, at any given moment. That is to say, we can only hold 7 ± 2 chunks of information in what Miller called 'immediate memory', which is now more usually referred to as 'working' or 'short-term' memory, at any one time. But just how much information is there in a 'chunk'?

As Miller himself explained, the simple answer is that there is no simple answer:

> the number of chunks of information is constant for immediate memory. The span of immediate memory seems to be almost independent of the number of bits per chunk, at least over the range that has been examined to date.

In practice, chunk size varies from person to person, and even from topic to topic. It also tends to grow in size as you become more familiar with the material. Just consider the following 'explanation':

> For VAT purposes, cross debit incomings and outgoings and enter the transaction in the day book and the residue in the bought ledger, unless the rolling annual total becomes negative, in which case record the transaction as an inverse credit payment, and enter the balance on an F11/789/K.

To the average person this paragraph contains at least eight chunks of information and probably looks quite genuine. An experienced bookkeeper, however, will see at a glance that the whole thing is sheer nonsense.

Picking the right level

Selecting the correct chunk size in a given situation, and knowing whether to chunk up or down – or both – are key skills in interpersonal communication.

No matter what the situation, if you chunk correctly you will have a significantly better chance of getting your message across. Choose the wrong chunk size, or chunk in the wrong direction, and you might as well stay at home.

Abstract mode

Someone in this mode is only interested in the big picture. Get too detailed and the *abstract* mode listener begins to switch off. If you really *must* go into details, then keep them as few and simple as possible, and make sure that you present them in an interesting or amusing way.

Abstract to specific mode

People in this group need the overview first in order to have a framework on which to hang the details which follow. Although they are willing to deal with a certain amount of detail, they have an instinctive feel (not necessarily infallible) for how much detail they need about a given subject. Once you cross this boundary – if you start to get *too* specific – then they are also likely to simply tune you out.

Specific mode

'But I did exactly what you asked. How was I to know the information was for a customer?' is typical of the sort of complaint made by someone in *specific* mode. They may be excellent at their particular job, whilst finding it difficult to relate what they do to the business of the department or company as a whole.

When taking on new information/skills people in *specific* mode like to have plenty of details, preferably with the underlying theory and some basic hands-on experience. Indeed, they may never feel ready to actually use a new skill until their knowledge is positively encyclopaedic (which is never).

Specific to abstract mode

This is the most practical of the four modes we've looked at. A person in this mode does need to get some detailed information in front of them when approaching a new activity, learning a new skill or whatever, but they are at least willing to use that information to work towards a synergistic understanding (that is, a view that is greater than the mere sum of the details).

People in this group are often seen as the backbone of a company. They're happy to do what they do day in and day out with commendable consistency, yet are capable of flashes of unexpected creativity if they are given the right encouragement – or even just because one little detail suddenly falls into place.

Why middle managers matter

Most senior managers and sales people work at 'big chunk' level, but the day-to-day operations of any business function mainly at the 'small chunk' level. A key function of an effective middle manager is to mediate between the two extremes. Companies which 'de-layer' too harshly can find that they are left with a serious communications gap.

Clearly, then, when going through the process of evaluating someone's skills, whether it be for recruitment or for promotion, it is important to assess whether that person is able to adjust their preferred information chunk size to the needs of each situation. The inflexible 'one size fits all' approach is seldom if ever appropriate in 21st century business.

Checkpoint actions

1. Check whether it's true that people usually chunk the information they give to other people using about the same chunk size that they would prefer when someone else is giving them information.
   a. When someone is giving you information, gauge how vague or precise they are being.
   b. Offer to check the information back to them, but when you do so be more precise or more vague.
   c. Does the other person correct you? Do the corrections mirror the chunk size they used before?
2. Select a topic on a subject you know well. Imagine that you are going to discuss this topic with two groups of people:
   a. Group A are familiar with the subject but not the topic.
   b. Group B have no relevant background knowledge of any kind. Break down the topic into 'chunks' suitable for each group and decide, in each case, whether you need to chunk up or chunk down for best effect.

16

What do you think?

I wonder...

Three important facets of NLP are:

1. asking questions;
2. knowing the right questions to ask; and
3. knowing when and how to ask them.

The main reasons for asking a question, in the context of NLP, are either (a) to get information, or (b) to get the person who is being asked the question to think about the answer.

The facts, ma'am, just the facts

The idea of asking questions to get information may seem rather obvious, until we look at it a little more carefully.

First of all, if we're asking for information that implies that this is something we don't yet have. But just because we don't have a particular piece of information doesn't automatically mean that we actually need it. Remember the example of the trip to London, in the last chapter. The point we were making was that the significance of a phrase like 'I'm going to London' was dependent on the context in which it occurred. If it was said by someone wanting to purchase a railway ticket for the journey then the ticket clerk would need some further clarification as to whether the traveller wanted to use a first class or a second class compartment, whether they wanted a single or a return, and so on. If the comment was made in passing during a conversation between friends or acquaintances, however, then the listener would be more likely to ask about the purpose of the trip (which would most likely be irrelevant to the ticket clerk), or they might simply take the statement at face value and not feel the need to ask any questions at all.

The point to be considered, then, is not simply 'Is there any information missing from what I am being told?' but rather 'Is there any information missing which I actually *need to know* (for whatever reason), and, if so, what *specifically* do I need to know that I haven't been told/shown so far?'

The meta model

The meta model was the earliest model created during the development of NLP. It is a linguistic model, largely based on Noam Chomsky's ideas on *Transformational Grammar* (John Grinder's particular field of interest and one on which he had co-authored a book in the period leading up to his collaboration with Richard Bandler).

In NLP jargon, linguistically ill-formed sentences are referred to as 'meta model violations'. Thus 'meta model violations' are not phrases which *violate* the meta model but the linguistic structures listed in the meta model. The basic underlying concept is that the words we use to create grammatically correct phrases and sentences (*surface structures*) only partially reflect the speaker or writer's underlying thoughts (*deep structures*).

In total, the meta model lists a dozen generic structures which appear meaningful but which actually conceal what the speaker is really thinking. Indeed, even the speaker may not realise what they are doing by using these structures. So when we ask the appropriate meta model question, we not only gain useful information; we may also help the speaker to consider the full implications of what they are saying. Five of the most commonly used meta model violations are:

- *Comparisons.* **The speaker makes a comparison but leaves out the basis for the comparison (a favourite advertising ploy). For example: 'This is the best laptop computer on the market.' To evaluate this claim we need to know 'Which market?' and 'By what yardstick is it "best"? On price, features, battery life per charge, or what?'**
- *Universal quantifiers.* **The speaker makes a sweeping generalisation, as in: 'The paperwork is never completed on time!' Since it is very unusual for anything to be *always* right, or *never* right, and so on, we need to ask the speaker if their generalisation really is universally applicable, as in: 'The paperwork has *never* been completed on time, not even once?'**
- *Unquestioned rules.* **The speaker cites the necessity to conform to a rule for which there is no better justification than something like: 'That's the way we've always done it.' Rather than question the rule itself we might ask questions designed to open up new possibilities, like: 'What other ways could this be done?' and 'What would happen if you did it another way?'**
- *Unspecified nouns.* **The speaker recounts an event using 'high level' descriptions instead of specific details, such as: 'Someone hurt themself in the machine shop.' This is hardly adequate for the health and safety record, and we need to ask: 'Who hurt themself? Give me their name.'**

- *Unspecified verbs*. The speaker recounts an event using a 'high level' verb, or verbs, instead of identifying specific actions. Using the previous example we also need to ask: 'How did this person hurt themself? What did they actually do?'

The full list of meta model violations also includes:

- *Cause and effect*. The speaker describes two events – A and B – as though event B is *caused* by event A. 'It makes me so angry when you are late.' (How does someone's behaviour control the speaker's emotions?)
- *Complex equivalence*. The speaker names two separate items and treats them as though they were the same thing. 'You didn't phone. What have I done wrong?' (How does not phoning imply that you've done anything wrong?)
- *Lack of referential index*. The speaker uses a pronoun instead of a name or title so that it is not clear who or what the speaker is talking about, for example the ubiquitous 'they', as in: 'They won't like it.' (Who are 'they'? What is 'it'?)
- *Lost performative*. The speaker delivers some kind of judgement without identifying the source. 'People should only express their opinions if they are well informed.' (Who says so?)
- *Mind reading*. The speaker assumes that whatever they think they know about what another person is thinking or feeling must be true: 'You want to make me look bad in front of the boss.' (What gave you that idea?)
- *Modal operator*. A word which implies an unspecified rule, such as: 'I *should* do abc' (modal operator of *necessity*), or which implies options, or a lack of options, such as: 'I *can't* do that' (modal operator of *possibility*).
- *Nominalisation*. The speaker refers to a process as though it were a static event, for example: 'Our relationship with this customer is not very good.'

(Which aspect(s) of the *interaction* between you and this particular customer are not satisfactory?)

- *Presupposition.* The speaker says something that assumes that a second, unspoken, statement is true when in fact it may *or may not* be true. For example: 'Don't cause any more trouble.' (Implies that the person *has* caused trouble at some time in the past.)
- *Simple deletion.* The speaker uses a sentence that is grammatically correct but omits some essential information, as in: 'Things have really started to improve!' (What, in particular, do you think has started to improve?)

Be gentle with me

When the meta model was first being developed, Bandler and Grinder found that their students were encountering considerable resistance when they asked the meta model questions straight out (as shown above), because they sounded more like an interrogation than simple requests for information.

It is better to couch the questions in a way that softens that interrogatory edge, as in:

- For mind reading: 'It's interesting you should say that. Was there anything in particular that gave you that idea?'
- For simple deletion: 'What would you say has improved the most?'

Telling without telling

The notion of asking someone a question in order to *tell* them something may seem a trifle bizarre, yet we actually do it quite regularly. That is to say, we ask a question in order to trigger an idea rather than because we want to hear the answer. And we can do it directly or indirectly. For example, lawyers really do ask witnesses questions which they know in advance will not get answered (a 'leading question', for example) and which, in all likelihood, the judge will order the jury to disregard. So why do they do it? They ask such questions because it allows them to put the relevant thought into the minds of the jury members – who, in most cases, will *not* disregard the question and may actually take *more* notice than if nothing had been said about it.

Using a question to make a point can be a more effective way of suggesting ideas, or drawing out the other person's thoughts, than making a direct statement. A question will normally put a convesation on 'hold' until the question is answered. A statement, on the other hand, doesn't *need* any response to make it complete. Likewise, a question, asked in a reasonable manner, is like a request, whereas even a perfectly innocuous statement can seem confrontational. The one draws out the listener's own view, whilst the other may seem to be telling the listener what they should think.

Checkpoint action

For best results: 'Practise (listening for evidence of missing information), Practise (deciding whether what's missing really matters), Practise (framing suitable questions to retrieve the missing information in a respectful manner).'

17

Avoiding resistance

I wanna tell you a story

Once upon a time the Khoja Nasruddin asked an architect friend to draw up plans for a modest town house.

'I've bought some land, and although I have no experience, I'm sure it can't be hard to build your own house. After all, if it were hard, there wouldn't be so many of them, would there?'

The architect, realising that his friend would not allow himself to be argued out of his intention, worked on the plans as requested, taking special care to make them as comprehensive and easy to follow as he possibly could.

About two weeks later the architect went down to the building site to see how things were getting on. He was amazed to find the Khoja standing beside a large stack of new bricks, with a mound of broken bricks on his other side.

He was even more amazed to see Nasruddin take a brick from the pile on his left and hit it with a hammer, then toss the pieces on to the mound of broken bricks on his right.

'What on earth are you doing?' asked the architect, 'You're destroying perfectly good bricks treating them like that.'

'Perfectly good bricks?' said Nasruddin, 'I don't think so. See how easily they break. The bricks with which I build my house will have to support a structure that weighs tons. I need to know whether the materials are good enough to do the job!'

The heart of the matter

Pierre Casse, a professor at the International Institute for Management Development in Lausanne, says, regarding the use of metaphors: 'When you hear a negotiator say, "*Oh, that reminds me of a story*..." – **be alert** – **at once...** a **story** is always dangerous in the sense that it is a **metaphor...**'

A metaphor, as Professor Casse explains, works on at least two levels. On the conscious level it is simply what it appears to be – an anecdote or fable. On the second level it allows us to talk to the subconscious mind in such a way that the conscious mind cannot censor or reject the underlying message(s).

In the story at the start of this chapter, for example, the overt message is a mild kind of joke.

But at a deeper level, the story has several messages, including:

- **Even an expert can't necessarily prevent a friend from making a fool of himself.**
- **Don't assume that a job is easy just because it's been done many times before.**
- **Logic becomes counterproductive when applied in an illogical manner.**

One word of warning before we move on: Because metaphors always carry indirect messages, anyone who hears the story, even if it was not meant for them, may hear a deeper meaning which you, the story teller, had never thought of or intended.

War is hell

You don't have to tell a whole story in order to use metaphors, of course. 'Time is money', 'a dog-eat-dog world', 'a cut-throat business' – these are all very meaningful metaphors of the type we hear around us every day. But how often do we stop to consider the consequences of using a particular set of metaphors?

How flexible can you be if you go into a negotiating session thinking 'We take no prisoners'? It doesn't fit with seeking win/win solutions, and is more likely to result in some major wins and some equally major losses, with not much in between.

NLP trainer Lara Ewing tells the story of a group of managers who were looking for appropriate metaphors to illustrate their individual roles within the company. As they went round the group one man introduced himself as 'The company fire-fighter'. The description sounded innocent enough at the time, but when the seminar was over another manager explained to Lara that the 'fire-fighter' included a metaphorical box of matches amongst his equipment. So if the gap between 'fires' seemed to be getting too long, the fire-fighter was liable to start one of his own in order to justify his existence!

Checkpoint actions

1. Watch how frequently people explain themselves with little stories. How does this affect your own understanding of what (you think) they are trying to say?
2. Use story-telling to enliven your own conversation, remembering that, in the business context, short stories work best.
3. What metaphors would you use to describe your company, the way it operates, and your main role within the company?
4. Listen out for the metaphors that your colleagues use in the work context. How accurate do you think they are?

18

Self-management

Do you mean what you say?

We've already discussed the relative importance of the words we say if they do not convey the same message given out by our vocal characteristics (tone, tempo, variability, etc) and our body language. If these three factors are not in accord – if we are not *congruent* – people will weigh up the message that they receive from each of the three forms of communication. (See FAQ 17 on my website at http://www.bradburyac.mistral.co.uk for a more detailed explanation.)

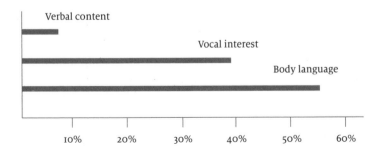

That's why we need to understand and manage our own *non-verbal* cues if we want our messages to be heard and *accurately* understood.

Values and beliefs

True congruence only occurs when we are behaving in complete accordance with our beliefs and values, working to a clear-cut and well-focused outcome, and when our words, vocal signals and body language are naturally synchronised.

Admittedly, much of life consists of making compromises, and achieving complete congruence is something of a struggle.

One way of achieving congruence is to push everything else to one side. Like a top-class athlete we can become so focused on the job in hand that nothing else intrudes upon our thoughts to distract us from achieving a particular outcome.

The strategy does have its limitations, however. In small doses it can be extremely effective, but if we make this our primary behaviour pattern over a protracted period of time we are likely to become – in other people's view – not congruent but 'obsessive', 'blinkered' and afflicted with 'tunnel vision'.

Congruence is a source of tremendous sustainable power, in the context of achieving outcomes. It is a way of being highly focused without becoming cold, ruthless or any of the other negative qualities we normally associate with an out-and-out go-getter. The solution is to maintain, as far as possible, an integrated posture by getting all of your *parts* to act in harmony.

A typical example of *incongruence* in the workplace is the person who values the social perks of belonging to a team, but also wants to be valued as an individual. Adept team leaders and managers ensure that their people get that recognition without having to act in a way which could disrupt the smooth running of the team.

The sum of the parts

Have you ever said something like: 'I think I agree, but part of me still isn't convinced'? According to NLP, when you talk this way – '*part* of me', 'I'm a *bit* worried', 'I'm not *entirely* sure' – it is something more than a mere figure of speech.

The 'bit' or 'part' is some portion of your subconscious which carries out a particular action or otherwise serves (or has served) some useful purpose. A typical 'part' is the 'little critic', the internal voice that serves a useful purpose by guiding us away from making careless mistakes, but which can also eat away at our self-confidence if it is constantly carping.

These parts are what we deal with in the *programming* aspect of NLP, and getting all of your parts to work together is the basis of a congruent posture. The more unanimity there is between the parts – the more congruent you are – the greater the potential for effective action.

Talking to parts

Imagine what it might be like to have a fear of heights. One part of you might say: 'I want to go to the 15th floor of this building to attend an important meeting', but if another part says: 'No way, that's much too high – I'm not going up there!', there is a distinct chance that you won't get to the meeting.

To achieve congruence you might do a deal with the part that is afraid of heights, such as: 'I'll go to the 15th floor but I won't watch the floor indicator in the lift, I won't look out of the windows, and I'll come back down as soon as I can.'

This is not to say that it is necessary to believe that your *self* is literally divided into hundreds of separate 'parts'. Like much of NLP, the concept of parts is simply a metaphor designed to convey an idea which works *as if* it were literally true.

It is possible, however, to have conversations with your

'parts', as the 'fear of heights' example suggested, and this can be very effective in a range of business situations.

The essential point is to recognise that the tensions that arise within us when we approach an important, new or emotionally charged experience (or any other experience, for that matter) are perfectly natural. The real question is: will we try to struggle through without resolving the tension – in a state of *in*congruence – or will we 're-program' our response to achieve a more harmonious, congruent and effective state?

Andrew Carnegie, self-made multi-millionaire and philanthropist, would often break off in the middle of a business meeting and go into another office by himself whilst he talked through the progress of the meeting, playing out the actions of everyone involved. Only when he was clear about his own position – his own outcome – would he rejoin the meeting.

> **Never negotiate with yourself in front of your competitors.**

We are naturally quite adept at recognising significant states of congruence or incongruence in other people. The phrase: 'I don't know why, he just made me feel uncomfortable' is a typical expression of this instinctive awareness.

'Need-to-know' management

A topic closely related to congruence is the practice of 'need-to-know'-style management: 'If you need to know, I'll tell you; if I don't tell you then you don't need to know.'

Of course, it is the right of management to release information 'at their own discretion'. But if it is impossible to know *everything* about even the simplest situation, how can we ever know in advance exactly what people will *need to know*? So, is a need-to-know policy really congruent with effective management and encouraging employees to act like responsible adults? Probably not.

Checkpoint action

We all talk to our 'parts' at some time or other, and these internal dialogues are perfectly natural. So get into the habit of listening to your inner voice. Learn to take advantage of your 'hidden depths', and take control of the 'little critic'.

19
Discipline

X, Y and NLP

According to Douglas McGregor, a professor of psychology at MIT, there are two basic styles of management.

Theory X

Managers who adopt Theory X do so on the assumption that:

- **Employees are naturally lazy, irresponsible and none too bright.**
- **It is management's task to direct, motivate and control employees according to the needs of the organisation.**

Theory Y

Managers following the Theory Y scenario assume that:

- **Employees already have motivation, a readiness to accept responsibility and the potential for self-development.**

- It is management's task to make it possible for people to achieve their own goals *best* by voluntarily directing their own efforts towards organisational objectives.

McGregor believed that the Theory Y assumptions encouraged positive behaviour, whilst Theory X managers were creating the very attitudes that they were complaining about. In other words, managerial style reflects managerial perceptions, and is likely to become self-fulfilling prophecy.

> From George's point of view, most of his staff are reasonably good workers – as long as he keeps an eagle eye on them. The real sore thumb is Mike, highly intelligent, good at his job, but (in George's opinion) totally lacking in social skills. Whenever there is trouble about, George takes it for granted that Mike will be involved somehow.
>
> As George has told his wife (several times), you can dream up all the theories you like, but at the end of the day the only way to deal with a person like Mike is to keep on top of him every moment of the day.

But is that really the best way to deal with 'difficult people'?

Problems and outcomes

NLP offers three vital observations which should be the foundation of every manager's portfolio of 'people skills':

- **People will always do the best they can with the resources available to them.**
- **Every behaviour has a positive intention behind it.**
- **Every behaviour is valid in some context.**

A company (or section, or department) where it is 'safe to make mistakes' is likely to foster greater employee loyalty, greater creativity and greater commercial success. Companies which run 'by the book', on the other hand, tend to be low in rapport, low in creativity and ultimately low in profitability.

So how can these presuppositions be put into practice?

Looking for problems

The 'traditional', 'tough', 'firm', 'no nonsense' style of management tackles 'problem' situations quite confrontationally by asking some version of the following five questions:

1. What is the problem?
2. How long has it been going on?
3. Whose fault is it?
4. Why hasn't someone done something about it?
5. Who is to blame (for not sorting it out)?

In the current example, this approach will surely indicate that Mike is at fault and George had better do something about it.

Now George can give Mike a good dressing down. But does this bring them any closer to a solution?

Outcomes that work

So far, not very good.

Maybe it's time to switch to Theory Y tactics? Unfortunately, as any experienced manager knows, there are some people who don't seem to respond to the Theory Y approach either.

NLP offers a third option based on studying the required outcome rather than simply restating the problem. This process starts with a very different set of questions:

1. What do you want?
2. What will be different when you have the desired result? (What will you see, hear and feel that will let you know that things have changed?)
3. What resources are already available to you which will help you to achieve the result you desire?
4. What other resources can you draw on?
5. What is the next step?

This new way of viewing the situation shifts from generalities to specifics, and from finding problems to finding answers:

1. Determine a suitable outcome (eg a smoothly running section with everyone getting on together).
2. Describe how things will be when the situation is resolved (a solution *does* exist and *will* be implemented).
3. When we accept that Mike is doing the best he can with the resources available to him then the first step is to find out what the situation looks like to Mike. Maybe he knows there is a problem and would jump at the chance of some help. On the other hand he may think that everyone else is at fault. Either way, it would be a good idea to find out what resources Mike himself can bring to the situation. (Assigning blame is as irrelevant to good management as finding fault. Does George want to find a solution – or simply make Mike's life uncomfortable?)
4. Depending on Mike's attitude, this step involves deciding what outside resources are needed, and who is going to provide them (Mike, the company or both)?
5. Finally, what are George and Mike actually going to do? (It is important that they arrive at a solution and start to implement it as soon as is reasonably possible.)

Not many managers are trained to look for outcomes by talking things through and giving guidance, and the whole process will undoubtedly take up more time and thought, as against simply making threatening noises. Still, it is a far more practical way of achieving effective solutions and the spread of coaching in business may encourage more use of this approach.

The alternative is well illustrated by an incident where a young woman had been accused of acting in a disruptive manner at work. The disciplinary procedure for this case involved six interviews, five managers, and at the end of the day the resulting 'written warning' gave no clear idea of how the young woman had breached company rules or what she was required to do next. Perhaps it wasn't so surprising then, that when the young woman wrote a letter to each manager involved, outlining ways in which she believed she could improve her social skills, only one person replied – three weeks later.

Would you estimate that the culture in that company is geared towards finding solutions, or towards finding problems (remembering that we usually find what we expect to find)?

Hidden commands

The phenomenon of inadvertent hypnosis, or subliminal commands (Chapter 12), is particularly relevant to the disciplinary procedure. Consider the following example:

> After being reprimanded over some matter, an employee was told by their manager: 'And if anything like this happens again it will be regarded as very serious indeed.'

This typical warning seems straightforward enough, yet it actually includes some very negative hidden messages:

- **'Since I'm issuing this warning about the next time, I clearly don't trust you to learn from this experience' (an implicit judgement – manager to employee).**
- **'I must keep watch on this person because I expect them to offend again' (the manager is effectively programming his future view of the employee).**

- 'Live up to my expectations – go and re-offend' (because this manager functions by giving orders, the warning becomes an implied command – manager to employee).

These messages have added power because they are effectively 'subliminal' (insinuated but not overtly stated) and therefore do not allow for an open discussion of their validity.

The fear of falling

Bullying, in whatever form, also has a subliminal foundation. That is to say, bullying invariably grows out of the bully's (unconscious and unadmitted) feelings of inadequacy and a fear of losing control rather than a direct wish to inflict pain and suffering on the person being bullied.

Employers who encourage a 'macho' culture, or are inclined to tolerate bullying – including overly severe and inflexible disciplinary procedures – may want to consider the negative consequences of such a culture on employee performance:

- Employees revert to 'tried and trusted' patterns of behaviour (bad for creativity and ability to handle change).
- Employees find it difficult to recognise underlying relationships and patterns in the work environment (bad for maintaining coherent activities).
- Employees show reduced powers of memory and 'higher order' thinking skills (bad for company performance).
- Employees tend to overreact to events in the workplace (bad for employee/employee, employee/customer and employee/management relationships).

Bullying is not only morally unacceptable; in the long term it can impair a company's ability to survive.

20

Appraisals

What's the point?

It might seem obvious that the yearly or half-yearly round of appraisal interviews best serves the needs of company and employees alike when the result is a more highly motivated workforce with a clear notion of how each person will raise their level of achievement in the year to come.

So isn't it strange that in so many companies the appraisal interview is surrounded by FUD – Fear, Uncertainty and Doubt!

> In an effective appraisal procedure, *both* parties are left with the sense that they have achieved a win/win result.

A key factor will be the ability of the appraiser to frame a clear outcome (Chapter 8), in which performance is measured against clearly defined, *mutually understood* expectations.

Perceptions and expectations

There is a famous experiment involving schoolteachers which shows very clearly how outcomes are moulded by our perceptions and our expectations (Chapter 3).

The teachers are told that a group of new students are either very eager and smart, or lazy and not very bright. In reality the students are selected so that the two groups are evenly matched, and about average in both attitude and ability.

As you may have guessed, the teacher who has been told that they are dealing with above average students, reports that their group are good workers and above average achievers. The teacher who thinks they are dealing with a group of problem students, however, finds that the students' behaviour, both personal and academic, is significantly below average.

Less easy to anticipate is the fact that many of the allegedly above average students actually do begin to achieve above average results, whilst some of the so-called underachievers begin to slip below their normal level of performance.

> **If you look for people's faults then, since none of us is perfect, you will certainly find much to criticise.**
>
> **If you look for the good in people then, since we generally strive to do the best we know how, with the resources available to us, you will certainly find much to praise.**

Onwards and upwards

As we've already said, an effective appraisal process must be based on positive, clearly defined, appropriate outcomes, having the intention of moving things 'onwards and upwards' rather than dwelling on the past.

Echoing a point made in the last chapter, three principles apply to all human behaviour:

- **People in a psychologically sound state of mind seldom if ever deliberately set out to fail or cause trouble.** So reviewing the past year to pick over the mistakes, and, worse yet, offering criticism without also providing concrete suggestions for improvement is, at best, pointless.

  The most realistic response to unwanted behaviour is to look for the good intention – and show the person how to achieve that intention in a more effective manner by helping them to become aware of a wider range of options.

- **A manager's job is to manage, ensuring that their subordinates have whatever resources they need to do their jobs. The difference between a poor manager and a good manager is often as simple as the difference between:**

  a. assuming that people '*should* know better', and
  b. helping each employee in whatever way is necessary for their success.

  It is interesting that some companies are now using staff appraisals as a way of assessing managerial performance.

- **Having a resource, knowing that you have that resource, and knowing how to use that resource can be three quite separate conditions. An effective appraisal will include:**

  - determining what resources an employee needs to fulfil their assignments, plus any resources they would like to possess (more or less relevant to their work[1]);

---

1 Various studies have shown that employee performance tends to be enhanced by learning in general –not only by the study of topics directly related to the company's main business.

- – **identifying those resources which the employee does not consciously possess;**
- – **drawing up a plan that will allow the employees to 'acquire' the additional resources, including on-the job experience, formal training, self-managed learning, etc.**

In short, the simple truth is that people succeed best when they are helped, encouraged and, above all, *allowed* to succeed.

21

Negotiations

Straight down the middle

A negotiation can be as immense in its purpose as a peace treaty between two nations, or as minor as discussing whether your child can have extra pocket money.

As long as the people on one side of the deal want something from the people on the other side of the deal, and both sides are willing to discuss the issues with the intention of reaching an agreement, then you have the basis for negotiation.

The negotiating process can be broken down into just five basic steps, which can be memorised using the mnemonic **PENCE:**

> **P**reparation
> **E**stimation
> **N**egotiation
> **C**onsummation
> **E**valuation

In other words, any serious negotiator will start by:

- **preparing his own position (step 1); and**
- **estimating the most likely position of the other party (step 2).**

These preparatory steps are followed by the actual negotiations (step 3), the decision either to reach an agreement or to agree to abandon the negotiation process (step 4), and the post-negotiation evaluation stage (step 5).

The preparation

The foundation of any good negotiating strategy is to have an unclouded view of your own outcome(s). Not just 'I want...', but clear definitions of:

1. your ideal outcome;
2. the outcome that you expect to arrive at (approximately);
3. the least satisfactory result that you are prepared to accept.

You may, in fact, draw up several different versions of step 3, in order of acceptability. These positions are often referred to as BATNAs (*best alternative to a negotiated agreement,* or *best alternative to non-agreement*).

The other man's shoes

It is also useful to get some idea of the position(s) the other party is likely to adopt. If you are dealing with a team you have faced before then this stage should be relatively easy. If they are complete unknowns, however, it can pay dividends to brainstorm the positions they *might* take, and work out your responses.

In both cases, however, you must bear in mind that you can never be entirely sure what someone is going to do until after they've done it. Whatever guesses you come up with, be prepared to throw every single one overboard, if necessary, once the negotiations start. This is a critical situation in which to exercise the presupposition that the person (or group) with the greatest number of choices will be most likely to achieve a satisfactory outcome.

How to cut a dovetail

The most successful negotiations are those where the two sides work together to reach a mutually acceptable outcome (a 'win/win' result).

To reach such a result you will need to establish good rapport (Chapters 9 to 11), and then introduce the notion of working as a partnership rather than staging a war of attrition. It may be a novel idea to some people, but if you have indeed established rapport then it should prove acceptable.

This 'dovetailing of outcomes' is made possible when both parties reach agreement on a point of common interest as the basis for the negotiations. It may be necessary to chunk up and down (Chapter 15) from your opening positions in order to find this common point, but it will be worth the time and effort in terms of reducing the number of red herrings and hidden agendas that pop up during the rest of the negotiating process.

Whilst sharing a common outcome can help negotiations along, do remember how fallible the human memory can be. In other words: work together, emphasise areas of agreement whenever they arise, and make sure that every point agreed on verbally is fully documented and signed. Do this as you go along, before people have had time to forget exactly what has been said.

Congruency and other ways to make a point

Staying congruent (Chapter 18) during the negotiating process is a very necessary skill. Well-constructed negotiating teams invariably include someone who operates in 'Differences' mode (Chapter 14) who will be particularly aware of any incongruence in both your team and in individual team members.

When you want to 'sell' a point, especially if you expect a certain amount of resistance, always state the reasons first and then follow up with the proposal (Chapter 13)

Metaphors

As described in Chapter 17, metaphors are an excellent way of getting your message across in a non-confrontational manner. They are also something to be regarded with the deepest suspicion when you are on the receiving end!

So how might you use metaphors in a negotiating situation? As a simple example, they can be used to indicate your own ideas about how the negotiating process should proceed:

> We had a situation like this not long ago, and the customer suggested that we do x, y and z, and sure enough we got the whole deal sewn up in next to no time. And everyone was totally satisfied with the result.

or to reject a proposal without making it personal:

> That reminds me of something I heard of just the other day. Someone over at ABC Ltd was telling me how one of their customers made a proposal much like the one you just put forward. The guys at ABC weren't entirely convinced that it was the best solution but they figured they were bound to respect the customer's decision. Come to think of it, Jerry was saying that it all ended in tears. Had to do the whole thing over from scratch. Still, that's life, I guess.

Notice that the positive stories are always about what 'we did', and the negative stories are always about someone else. This way you can give 'advice' without seeming to be saying '*we* knew best, but *they* wouldn't listen', and you and/or your company appear to be the epitome of reasonable co-operation.

Specify to clarify

Just how often do we send or receive generalised statements as though they were precise descriptions (Chapter 15)? As Kepner and Tregoe observed in their book The Rational Manager:

> With management growing progressively more complex, and experience more obsolete more rapidly, the manager must rely more and more on skilful, rational questioning, and less and less on experience.

This was written not, as you might imagine, in the 1980s or 1990s, but as far back as 1965. Yet it points up a problem that is as real now as it was over 40 years ago.

It's not clear whether we just don't like asking questions, so we never learn to do it well; or whether the widespread lack of effective questioning skills leads us to suppose that this does not fall within the range of learnable skills. Thus we continually fall into this kind of trap:

> **A:** 'We must have guaranteed delivery by the end of June.'
> **B:** 'No problem.'

Two months later:

> **A:** 'Your delivery was late!'
> **B:** 'No it wasn't. The goods reached you at 12.30 pm on the thirtieth of June!'
> **A:** 'That's what I mean. We said "by" the end of the month, not "at" the end of the month.'

Yet this is entirely unnecessary. There is a simple, three-step approach to questioning that allows us to be precise and accurate without resorting to something akin to interrogation:

1. Spot when details are missing.
2. Differentiate between essential and non-essential details.
3. Ask the right questions the right way to uncover the missing details (see the meta model questions in Chapter 16).

And a few points to remember when asking questions:

- If you ask a question that starts with 'why?' be sure to present it in a reasonable tone. People don't like to be interrogated.
- With 'open' and 'closed' questions, research shows that there is, in fact, no fixed rule as to which form is most likely to get the most detailed response. So that if you aren't getting the details you need there's nothing wrong with asking what lawyers would call a leading question, along the lines of: 'So, can you help me with some details here – what did you actually tell the customer?'
- Once you've asked the question, really listen to the answer – the whole answer. Firstly because it will increase rapport, and secondly because the other person may not be saying what you initially think they are saying.
  Teacher: Mary, give me a sentence beginning with 'I'
  Mary: I is ...
  Teacher: No, no, Mary. That should be 'I am ...'
  Mary: Yes, Miss. I am the ninth letter of the alphabet.
  Accept the answers you get in a reasonable manner, whether you like them or not. A response like 'You did what!?' can cut a potentially useful session stone dead.

Be willing to keep asking questions until you get the answers you really need. Most people aren't used to giving 'rational' answers because they aren't used to being asked 'rational' questions.

22

Meetings

What are we here for?

As we've seen throughout this introduction to NLP, it is relevant
to every area of business activity, for the simple reason that
communication, of one sort or another, is at the heart of all
business activities.

It would be easy, then, to write a complete book just on the
application of NLP in meetings. Unfortunately, we don't have
room to do that, so this chapter will concentrate on the six major
steps that comprise any meeting – always assuming that a
meeting is the best way of achieving your outcome(s):

- **Direction.**
- **Evidence.**
- **Confirmation.**
- **Observation.**
- **Review.**
- **Agreement.**

Decide on the direction

Generally speaking, the agenda for a meeting indicates the topics to be discussed, but it does little or nothing to ensure the success of that meeting.

When we talk about the outcome(s) (Chapter 8) for a meeting, we're interested in what the discussion will lead to – the 'direction' it will take, not just where it starts out. In this way we give the meeting focus and direction, and avoid the all too common problem of entering into inevitably fruitless discussions. (This will normally be decided on when the agenda is being drawn up – before the meeting takes place.)

Agree the evidence

There is a widely held belief that discussing what has to be done is a time-wasting exercise and the way to succeed is simply to 'get stuck in'. A number of studies have shown that this is simply not true. Indeed, it is possible to cut the total time taken to achieve a given result by as much as a third simply by discussing the task before any action is taken.

So discussing outcomes at the very start of a meeting is far from a waste of time. Likewise there is value in agreeing how you will (jointly) know when you have satisfactorily achieved those outcomes *before* you actually try to reach any agreement. (Unless there is a very good reason for doing otherwise, the evidence should also be decided on whilst the agenda is being prepared.)

Confirm the outcome(s)

The third step in the opening of a meeting is to check that you've all caught the same bus. That is to say, you should now summarise and confirm the outcomes that have been agreed upon, and what will have to be true in order to know that those outcomes have been achieved. This will be far more successful if the items in question are written down and circulated. If possible they should be sent out and photocopied whilst the meeting continues.

Observations

Throughout the course of the meeting, be alert to what is really going on (that is, be aware of what people do – don't depend on what they say). If someone says they agree on a particular point, but shows non-verbal evidence of confusion or doubt, be sure to deal with those non-verbal cues (Chapter 6) before the meeting closes or the agreement you have reached may not last.

Do remember that different people have different convincer modes (Chapter 14) – one agreement does not (necessarily) a deal make.

Review important decisions

Make sure that all important decisions reached in the course of the meeting are reviewed and agreed.

The results of the review can then be recorded in summarised form, which has the added advantage of being a good way of checking that you all agree not just on the wording but also on the meaning of each decision.

Agree action(s)

And finally, agree on the action to be taken on the basis of the decisions that have been made. These actions should feature in the minutes when they are circulated to the participants so that everyone knows what's going on, who has responsibility for the various follow-up actions, and any disputes can be aired (and settled) as quickly as possible.

Challenge for relevance

Whenever (if ever) a meeting seems to be losing focus because someone is (in your opinion) going into too much detail, taking too broad an overview, or simply diverging from the point, be confident enough to firmly and politely challenge the speaker to explain what relevance their point has to the agreed outcome(s) for the meeting.

Having said that, do remember to challenge the point, not the person making the point. The aim is to keep the meeting on track, not to create friction. Remember, every action has a positive intention, and even the most irritating nit-picker may have a valid point to make.

23

Presentations

Who are you talking to?

One of the worst, and most common, mistakes made by presenters is to assume that the most important element in a 'good' presentation is a well-constructed argument. Wrong! The best foundation for *any* presentation is to establish and maintain rapport with your audience. Like every other aspect of communication, what happens at the non-verbal level is often far more important to the success of a presentation than any amount of clever scripting.

This does not remove the need for good scripting as well as good rapport skills. The point is that people won't take full notice of you without adequate rapport, not that lack of rapport will cause them to be miraculously struck deaf.

In a superficial sense, presentations come in all shapes and sizes, from a one-to-one training session up to a major bells and whistles and coloured lights multimedia event. To some extent, then, the way you handle a particular presentation – what visual aids you use, and so on – should reflect the size and purpose of the event. But that, too, is secondary to the job of creating the bond between the audience and yourself.

The following list shows five elements that are applicable to *any* presentation, which form the rather appropriate mnemonic OSCAR:

clear	**O**utcome
layered	**S**tructure
selective	**C**hunking
positive	**A**ttitude
flexible	**R**esponse

Outcome

No presentation is going to be successful if it doesn't have a clearly defined outcome, or set of outcomes – at least one for you and one for your audience (Chapter 8). For example:

- **I want to give a brief and powerful presentation of three key reasons why my new product idea should be accepted for manufacture.**
- **I want the people at the presentation to support my proposal and feed in any ideas they may have for improvements.**

These outcomes should be clearly detailed at the start of the event, and adhered to: 'I'm going to describe three key reasons why this product should go into production. In addition to the details I'm going to set out for you, I'm really interested in getting any ideas you may have for improving on the basic specification.'

This approach quickly puts the audience at ease because they no longer have the feeling that they must blindly follow wherever you choose to lead. It also provides a framework which will make it easier for your audience to understand and remember the points made during the presentation.

Structure

In order to effectively utilise preferred thinking styles (Chapter 5) and meta programs (Chapters 14 and 15), take extra care over the *structure* of your presentation. Switch frequently, but not obviously, from one rep' system to another throughout the presentation. And take care to cater to whichever meta programs you think are relevant (towards–away from, sameness–difference, etc). By addressing appropriate meta programs you are telling people in the most direct way possible: 'This is for *you*!'

Chunking

Also on the subject of meta programs, be sure to 'chunk' your material (Chapter 15) so as to retain audience interest.

Since each member of your audience will have their own preferences, your best option is to choose a middle-of-the-range starting point, and then chunk up. Allow questions from the audience so that people can ask for more detail if they wish, but avoid getting bogged down in 'nitty-gritty' details (unless that level of detail is a necessary element of the event).

Attitude

This means more than simply 'think positive'. Effective presenters share an unusually high level of self-confidence, at least whilst they are delivering a presentation. It is as though they will the event to succeed by their unflagging belief in that success, a belief that will be conveyed to and impressed upon the audience through a variety of non-verbal signals.

Response

There are at least three positions from which you can view any situation – your own, the other person's standpoint, and that of an impartial observer. In NLP these are known as first, second and third position, respectively.

The fifth quality that contributes to a truly impressive presentation style is a mixture of sensitivity and flexibility. Top presenters constantly switch back and forth between viewpoints, always aware of the response they are getting from their audience, and able to customise the presentation as they go in order to achieve their desired outcome.

'Anchoring the room'

A question that comes up regularly in presentation skills courses is: 'Should I move about and, if so, how much?'

In practice this isn't quite the right question. For someone who feels comfortable staying relatively still, it would be a mistake to start pacing around 'because they should'. And for someone who feels comfortable moving around, it would be equally wrong to restrict their movements too much.

A more useful consideration is how moving around during a presentation – by 'anchoring the room' – can be used to good effect.

This technique is based on the idea that if we repeat certain actions in a consistent manner then we can use the actions as non-verbal signals to give the presentation an additional structure.

As a simple example, suppose I consistently move between three positions – stage left, centre stage and stage right. And suppose I only move to one of those positions when I come to particular points in my presentation. When I have an important fact to convey I move to the left side of the stage. When I'm presenting less important linking material I go to stage centre. And on the occasions when I want to be light-hearted I position myself on the right-hand side of the stage.

After I've done this a few times most members of the audience will understand, though probably unconsciously, what it signifies when I move to one or another of the three positions and will be more in tune with my message as a consequence.

24

Sales

It's the way that you do it

'Differentiation' – the crucial art of making your own product or service stand out from all of its (very similar) rivals seldom has much to do with the product as such. When you are competing in a market full of nearly identical products there's little mileage in stressing the negligible differences between one product and another. It is usually better to concentrate on the 'halo' around your product – the associations which will make that item or service *appear* to be more desirable.

Most people, the CEOs to receptionists, are essentially creatures of habit. They develop certain buying patterns, which are unlikely to change without a very good reason. And the reason is likely to be personal rather than business-oriented. (In a recent study, 76 per cent of the companies that changed suppliers had done so because the relationship with the supplier's rep had broken down in some way.)

However unbusinesslike it may seem, in a selling situation developing rapport with the customer matters far more than mere technical details (Chapters 9–11).

Believe it or not, the fact that your product or service is genuinely superior to everything else on the market is not necessarily your customer's primary concern.

To tell or not to tell

As we saw in Chapter 3, everyone has their own 'world view', which means that any person you are selling to will have their own individual set of reasons for buying – or not buying – whatever it is you are selling.

So, if you go into a selling situation and immediately start to tell the customer about your product or service (hereafter I'll use the word 'product' to refer to both) then you will be selling, at best, to some mythical 'Mr Average', or at worst, to yourself. That is to say, you will be telling the customer what you believe they *ought* to want to hear, or you will be telling them what *you* would want to hear.

In neither case are you treating the customer as a real person.

> **The person asking the questions controls the conversation.**

Features and benefits

In order to enter your customer's world, which is where the sale will actually take place, you must ask questions which will encourage the customer to tell you what you really need to know (Chapter 8). In addition to the questions given there you can use simple and precise questions relating to the customer's previous buying experiences. These questions need to be simple and precise, such as:

'What did you like most about your last fleet car supplier?'
'Is there any way in which they could have given better service?'
'What did you least like about XYZ Training Ltd?'
'In what way did they fail to meet your training needs?'

Once you have a clear idea of what the customer actually wants from the product that you are selling, you can frame your sales pitch to show how specific 'features' of your product can *benefit* the customer by answering specific needs. Incidentally, if you can't match a particular need, or if there are features of your product which don't relate to any of the customer's declared needs, *leave that information out of your presentation*. No matter how many wonderful bells and whistles your product may have, the customer will only buy, and be satisfied with, what the *customer* actually wants.

How, then, can you help the customer to find out what they really want? Think representational systems.

Selling to visual mode customers

Even when you think you know what they want, trying to *tell* a customer or client what your product can do for them, when they are in visual mode, will be a total waste of time – unless you paint 'word pictures' for them. A customer in visual mode wants to *see* what they're getting for their money, be it a car, a holiday, a new pair of shoes or a computer upgrade.

Be patient going in to the sale – a person in visual mode often wants to literally *view* all the alternatives before making a final decision. Give them the time they want, and don't try to talk to them until they mention something like a 'shortlist', at which point you can help the process along by asking questions that stimulate visual images:

'Can you see yourself lying on that beautiful golden beach?'

'The hi-tech styling really works well on this CD player, doesn't it?'

'Just imagine the other drivers trying not to stare as you glide down the motorway in this beauty.'

When a customer in visual mode does come to a decision, they usually do so quickly and with conviction (they have finally built a mental picture which looks right). Avoid chitchat. If you disturb that mental image you may literally talk yourself out of a sale.

Finally, if a customer in visual mode isn't ready to make an on-the-spot commitment, make sure you give them some kind of visual reminder to take away with them.

Selling to auditory mode customers

You might think that the best way to sell to customers in auditory mode would be by talking about your product. In practice however, it is the customer who will usually want to do the talking, at least in part because they often do not know exactly what they are thinking until they hear themselves say it out loud.

As soon as a person in auditory mode begins to interrupt or raise their voice you know that they have started an internal review of the sale. Listen carefully and they will tell you everything you need to know to complete a mutually satisfactory transaction – nuggets such as when they last made a similar purchase, and, even more importantly, what triggered their decision on that previous occasion.

Be prepared to answer questions, but remember that the most effective salesperson for someone in auditory mode is their own voice. If they start to repeat themselves then the sale probably isn't happening. In this case listen carefully to what they are saying (to find out where they are 'stuck'), then reframe the barrier (Chapter 13) to allow the sale to progress.

Selling to kinaesthetic mode customers

Making a sale to a customer or client who is in kinaesthetic mode can be very easy and very difficult – and both in the same transaction.

The process is easy in so far as people in kinaesthetic mode are concerned, because they readily respond to emotionally charged presentations and to 'hands-on' experience of the product – as long as the salesperson's enthusiasm doesn't become a hustle.

However, whilst a person is in kinaesthetic mode they will tend to buy in response to their feelings, and may change their mind about a purchase just as soon as the accompanying emotion fades away. If this happens they may not necessarily regret having bought the item (although they are the group most likely to suffer from 'buyer's remorse'). Rather they will start to question whether they got a good deal, whether the purchase was really necessary, and so on. (This indecision is even more likely if anyone questions them about their purchase.)

In order to minimise the effects of this 'aftershock' syndrome, it is necessary to provide built-in reassurance.

IBM used to have a slogan along the lines of:

No one ever got fired for buying IBM.

True or not, the effect of the slogan was to reassure people who were in kinaesthetic mode that they had made the right choice by redirecting their fears towards the possible consequences of any alternative action (ie buying from our competitors *could* seriously damage your career).

Likewise, the documentation that accompanies many

electrical goods congratulating the customer on their wise choice and asking them to register for after-sales support is an excellent way of reassuring people in kinaesthetic mode, and impulse buyers that they have made the right decision.

Selling to groups

But do these guidelines work *with groups*? In fact, the approach is equally valid in both situations since a group is composed of individuals, so you still need to deal with individual rep' systems. The difference when dealing with a group is that you need to use your sensory acuity to identify the key member(s) of the group (eg decision makers), and identify their currently most active rep' system(s) (Chapter 5). Then target your presentation accordingly.

Look for the person or people who seem most at ease, who clearly are not afraid to express an opinion, who are the focus of attention for the rest of the group, and so on. If you're still not sure who the key figures are, simply tailor your presentation to cover all three rep' systems more or less equally. In this manner you're bound to be on the same wavelength with everyone in the audience at some time or other. It's not very scientific, but it's better than achieving no rapport at all.

More NLP resources including more detailed descriptions of the NLP presuppositions and meta programs, can be found on the author's website http://www.bradburyac.mistral.co.uk

25

Training

Choosing an NLP trainer

I am often asked, through my website, to recommend an NLP trainer or training company. Unfortunately there are a lot of very poor quality courses on offer, and many trainers who seem to have little idea what authentic NLP is all about.

Based on my own experience, to the first question I always answer: John Grinder (co-creator of NLP with Richard Bandler and therefore one of the only two 100 per cent experts on NLP). And for training in the UK I recommend Michael Carroll's NLP Academy. Michael is a first rate trainer in his own right, and Michael, John Grinder and John's co-trainer, Carmen Bostic St Clair, have jointly set up the International NLP Academy which offers various courses, from NLP Practitioner upwards, including specialist courses on storytelling, 'pattern hunting' (an advanced application of NLP skills), and so on.

The NLP Academy is located in Croydon, just outside London in the UK. For full details of their courses go online to http://www.nlpacademy.com, or contact them at:

NLP Academy
The Pavillions, 35 Brighton Road,
Croydon, Surrey, CR2 6EB
Tel: +44 (0) 208 686 9952

Basic NLP terms used in this book

(Words in italics are described elsewhere in the list of terms.)

Anchor   An 'anchor' is a link between an internal *state* and an external stimulus (eg a piece of music that recalls a past event).

Anchoring   The process of creating an *anchor*. Anchors can be created deliberately or by chance. They can also be altered and even removed ('dissolved').

As if
1. An event can be dealt with through visualisation 'as if' it had actually happened.
2. There is proven value in adopting certain presuppositions 'as if' they were true, even though it hasn't been proved that they are universally true.

Associated   To be 'associated' with a given event or memory is to view it as someone taking part in that event. (See also *Dissociated*).

Auditory mode   Using sound as the PTS
(See also *Kinaesthetic mode* and *Visual mode*.)

Beliefs   An idea about some aspect of ourselves or the external
world which we hold to be true without having any objective
supporting evidence – 'I've never tried it, I just know [*believe*]
I won't like it.'
(See also *Values*.)

Chunk   One or more items of information which a given person
can handle as a single concept or idea.

Chunking
1. Dividing a large piece of information into smaller
'chunks'.
2. Moving from details to generalities ('chunking up') or vice
versa ('chunking down').

Congruence (external)   External congruence exists when your
body language, vocal signals and verbal message all send the
same message.
Being externally congruent is closely related to your level of
internal congruence.

Congruence (internal)   Internal congruence exists when you
are completely focused on the task in hand *and* you are at
ease about the situation (ie when all of your 'parts' are in
harmony).

Conscious   That part of the mind which is immediately
accessible. It is the conscious mind which can only hold
seven items of information, plus or minus two.

Content   In any communication, the 'content' is the message
you are giving out – as distinct from other people's
interpretation of your message.
(See also *Process* and *State*.)

Crossover mirroring   Indirectly matching another person's body language – you scratch your neck, I rub my arm – usually as part of the process of establishing rapport.

Deletion   The process of ignoring certain items of information about some event or person (for *any* reason).

Dissociated   To be dissociated from an event or memory is to view it as though watching it as an observer. (See also *Associated*.)

Distortion   The process of reshaping information so that it misrepresents external reality (for *any* reason).

Dovetailing (outcomes)   Matching your outcome with some one else so that both outcomes can be achieved as far as this is possible. Note that dovetailing implies reaching a reasonable compromise but does not require you to sacrifice your own interests in favour of the other party.

Frame   The context within which a person, thing or event is *perceived*.

Generalisation   The process of creating a general rule or assumption on the basis of a very limited amount of evidence.

Kinaesthetic mode   Using feelings – physical and/or emotional – as the primary information processing sense. (See also *Auditory mode* and *Visual mode*.)

Leading   Doing something different from the person with whom you are communicating, usually after a period of *pacing*.

Matching   Discreetly copying someone else's body language as part of the process of creating and maintaining *rapport* (you cross your arms – I cross my arms, etc).

Mental map   In this context, a mental representation of a person, event or thing. All mental maps are, by definition, incomplete and out of date. Nevertheless, they are the best information we have about 'reality'.

Meta program   An internal filter used to process incoming information and determine an appropriate reaction.

Metaphor   A story – based or partly based on real or entirely fictional events – designed to convey a message so that it will be more readily received by the listener.

Mirroring   Synonymous with *matching*.

Modal operators   Internal rules by which people govern their own behaviour and judge the behaviour of others.

Modelling   A basic NLP skill, in this context modelling is the process of capturing the thoughts and actions which distinguish an expert in some field from someone who is merely competent. The information must be described in such a way that it is possible for other people to replicate the relevant elements in order to enhance their own skill level.

Outcome (well-formed) A goal or want which has been

- **consciously and specifically defined in positive terms; and**
- **can be achieved by the individual setting the outcome with minimal external help; and**
- **has no discernible detrimental consequences.**

Pacing   *Matching* and *mirroring* another person's body language to help build rapport, often prior to *leading* (see above).

Perceptions   Our conscious view of the external world. Our perceptions are often shaped by our *beliefs*, *values* and expectations.

Process   In any communication, the 'process' element is the way that you handle your side of the communication.

Rapport   A state of mutual trust and respect existing between two or more people. Rapport is the primary basis for all successful communications.

Reality (external)   The totality of the universe outside our skins. Since nothing is completely knowable our view of external reality is always limited.

Reality (internal)   Internal reality is what is 'real' to a given individual – their current *mental map* of external reality.

Reframe   Re-stating a view of *reality* (internal or external), usually in order to make it easier to deal with.

Representational Systems   The five sensory systems we use to take in and process information about the external world – visual, auditory, kinaesthetic, gustatory and olfactory.

Resource   Any internal quality (confidence, humour, calmness, etc) which makes it easier to perform a required task. Having a resource does not necessarily mean that we know that we have it, and even when we know that we have a particular resource we may still need time and guidance to learn how to use it effectively.

Resourceful state   Being aware that you have, and know how to use, the *resources* required in a given situation.

Sensory acuity   The skill of being sensitive to a person's nonverbal changes (rate of speech, skin colour, muscle tension, etc), which give clues to their mental activity.

State   Your actual condition (emotional, physical and mental), appropriate or otherwise, at any particular moment.

Thinking (multiple choice) Thinking based on the (usually correct) view that there are as many options as you can think of – and then some.

Thinking (two-valued) Thinking based on the (usually incorrect) assumption that there are only two options in a given situation.

Ultradian rhythm A naturally occurring pattern of alternating consciousness, consisting of approximately 90 minutes of normal awareness followed by about 20 minutes of semi-trance-like consciousness. The rhythm continues throughout both day and night, except that at night the 90 minute periods are spent in normal sleep, whilst the 20 minute periods are generally when REM (rapid eye movement) sleep and dreaming take place.

Unconscious The part of your mind which you are usually not aware of. The unconscious mind can handle vast amounts of information and multiple activities simultaneously.

Values Filters we use to evaluate incoming messages about ourselves and the world around us – good/bad, worthwhile/worthless, and so on. Our values are normally closely tied to our *beliefs*.

Visual mode Using sight as the primary information processing sense.
(See also *Auditory mode* and *Kinaesthetic mode*.)

Other titles in the Kogan Page Creating Success series

The above titles are available from all good bookshops. For further information on these and other Kogan Page titles, or to order online, visit the Kogan Page website at **www.koganpage.com**